Standardized Test Preparation Workbook

Grade Eight

Upper Saddle River, New Jersey
Boston, Massachusetts

Copyright © by Pearson Education, Inc., publishing as Pearson Prentice Hall, Boston, Massachusetts 02116. All rights reserved. Printed in the United States of America. This publication is protected by copyright, and permission should be obtained from the publisher prior to any prohibited reproduction, storage in a retrieval system, or transmission in any form or by any means, electronic, mechanical, photocopying, recording, or likewise. For information regarding permission(s), write to: Rights and Permissions Department, One Lake Street, Upper Saddle River, New Jersey 07458.

Pearson Prentice Hall™ is a trademark of Pearson Education, Inc.
Pearson® is a registered trademark of Pearson plc.
Prentice Hall® is a registered trademark of Pearson Education, Inc.

ISBN 0-13-190797-2

2 3 4 5 6 7 8 9 10 06 07 08

Contents

© Pearson Education, Inc., publishing as Pearson Prentice Hall. All rights reserved.

Name ______________________ Date ______________

Screening Test

Directions: Read the following passages. Then answer the questions. On the answer sheet, fill in the bubble for the answer that you think is correct.

Telephones, faxes, and computers are company property and should be used for company business only. This includes voice mail, electronic mail, and computer files. Employees may need to use these communication tools for personal reasons from time to time. If and when that time comes, employees should keep their personal use to a minimum and should do so only during non-work hours such as lunchtime.

1 According to the passage, which of the following is *true*?

A Employees can use computers for personal use only.
B Employees are never allowed to use computers for personal reasons.
C Employees should keep their personal use of computers to a minimum.
D Employees cannot use computers during their non-work hours.

2 When are employees at this company allowed to use the telephone for personal reasons?

F when work is slow
G when taking an official break
H whenever they need to
J whenever their boss approves

3 This paragraph describes —

A how to use computers for personal reasons
B how to fix a fax machine
C the rules for taking a lunchtime break
D the rules for using office communication tools

To Start Your Washer:
1. Measure detergent and add to basin.
2. Set water temperature control and number of rinses.
3. Close lid and pull wash cycle knob out to begin washing.

4 What information do you find in this passage?

F descriptions of temperature settings for a washer
G speeds and controls for a washer
H directions for starting a washer
J instructions for care and service of a washer

5 What is the first step in using the washer?

A setting the water temperature
B setting the number of rinses
C pulling the wash cycle knob
D measuring detergent and adding it to the basin

6 What should you do immediately before pulling the wash cycle knob?

F measure the detergent
G set the number of rinses
H close the washer lid
J add the detergent to the basin

© Pearson Education, Inc., publishing as Pearson Prentice Hall. All rights reserved.

Name ______________________________ Date ______________

What could chocolate and Coca-Cola possibly have in common? Both contain caffeine and are popular around the world. The main ingredient in chocolate comes from the beans of the cacao tree, and the flavoring for Coca-Cola originally came from the nuts of the kola tree. Although they grow in different parts of the world, the cacao tree and the kola tree are part of the same plant family.

7 One ingredient chocolate and Coca-Cola have in common is —

A kola nuts
B caffeine
C cacao beans
D cocoa

8 Chocolate's main ingredient —

F grows in a different part of the world than Coca-Cola's flavoring
G is more popular around the world than Coca-Cola's flavoring
H is derived from a different plant family than Coca-Cola's flavoring
J is less popular around the world than Coca-Cola's flavoring

1 "Who's that?" asked Jamey.

2 Karyn looked at the tall, athletic woman with gray hair tied back in a short ponytail. "Oh, that's my grandmother. She's training for the City Run next week."

3 The two girls finished their run and sat on the sidelines. The older woman joined them shortly.

4 "How's it going, Nanna?" Karyn asked.

5 "Pretty good," her grandmother replied. "I cut three seconds off my best time."

6 Jamey looked at the older woman. "How long have you been running?" she asked.

7 "Most of my life," Nanna replied. "But not on a team. You girls are lucky."

8 "What do you mean?" Jamey asked, confused.

9 Nanna told the girls about the old days when women had few opportunities to race. She explained how things changed when Kathryn Switzer entered the Boston Marathon in 1967. "She registered as K. Switzer so no one would know she was a woman," Nanna said. "She finished in four hours and 20 minutes, better than some men."

10 Nanna rose to her feet and said good-bye to the girls. The girls watched Nanna as she jogged to the parking lot. "Your grandma is pretty cool," Jamey said.

9 What causes Karyn to look over at the woman who was running?

A The woman is running fast.
B Jamey asks who the woman is.
C Karyn is looking for another friend.
D The woman is talking about Kathryn Switzer.

10 What effect do you think meeting Nanna will have on Jamey?

F She will like Karyn more as a friend.
G She will want to enter the Boston Marathon.
H She will appreciate being able to participate in sports.
J She will come back to the track more often.

© Pearson Education, Inc., publishing as Pearson Prentice Hall. All rights reserved.

Name ______________________ Date ______________

1 Rebecca moved around in her seat nervously. Her teacher had asked the students to give oral reports on family history. All the students had wonderful stories. Robbie said his great-grandfather had been a cowboy. Angelica's ancestors had come from Ireland on a ship.

2 When her turn came, Rebecca rose slowly and walked to the front of the class. She took a deep breath and began. "My family is from Germany," she started. "They were Jewish, and in the 1930s, Adolf Hitler and the Nazis were rounding up Jews and putting them in work camps."

3 She told of how her great-grandparents decided to flee to America. "They had to walk to Germany's border," Rebecca said. "It was more than a hundred miles. They traveled at night and slept during the day. It was very hard."

4 Rebecca held up a tiny doll. "My grandmother carried this in her pocket for weeks. It's still dirty from the trip because my grandmother never washed it. She said that it reminded her of what she and her family endured for freedom."

5 The class was silent for a moment, then the students asked many questions about Rebecca's story and her family. At that moment, the butterflies in Rebecca's stomach were replaced with a glow of pride. The teacher's encouraging smile told her that she had helped her classmates learn about courage.

11 What is this story *mostly* about?

A a teacher who asks her students to give reports

B a girl who tells how her family came to America

C a class of students who have nice stories

D why some people tried to escape from the Nazis

12 What is the main idea of the last paragraph?

F The teacher decides that Rebecca needs help.

G The class doesn't understand Rebecca's story.

H Students often ask too many questions about families.

J Rebecca changes from being afraid to feeling proud.

13 Which of these is a *fact* from the story?

A The teacher had asked the students to give oral reports.

B Adolf Hitler and the Nazis were rounding up Jews and putting them in work camps.

C Rebecca rose slowly and walked to the front of the class.

D all of the above

14 Which of these is an *opinion* in the story?

F Rebecca moved around in her seat nervously.

G All the students had wonderful stories.

H Rebecca's great-grandparents decided to flee to America.

J Rebecca held up a tiny doll.

© Pearson Education, Inc., publishing as Pearson Prentice Hall. All rights reserved.

Name ______________________ Date ______________

One of the most breathtaking places in the world, the Grand Canyon, lies in northwestern Arizona. It is about 277 miles long, 1 mile deep, and anywhere from 1 to 18 miles wide. In 1869, an American geologist named John Wesley Powell led a river expedition through the canyons of the Green and Colorado Rivers. Powell named the area the Grand Canyon, and his exploration of the area was one of the greatest adventures in American history. Few people remember Powell today, but he and his fellow explorers accomplished an extraordinary feat that would be difficult even with today's technology.

15 Which of the following statements is *not* supported by the paragraph?

A John Wesley Powell was lazy.
B John Wesley Powell was curious.
C John Wesley Powell was brave.
D John Wesley Powell was determined.

16 After reading this paragraph, Connie thinks that a trip through the Grand Canyon would be harder than she first thought. Which words from the story cause her to think this?

F ". . . feat that would be difficult even with today's technology."
G "One of the most breathtaking places in the world . . ."
H "Powell named the area the Grand Canyon . . ."
J ". . . Powell led a river expedition through the canyons . . ."

Directions: Read the following questions. On the answer sheet, fill in the bubble for the answer that you think is correct.

17 Which of these describes poetry?

A Facts are presented so that you can understand them easily.
B The setting is described in great detail.
C Stage directions show the placement of characters.
D Rhyme and rhythm help you understand the meaning.

18 What is a great advantage of writing fiction?

F You can write about things that haven't happened.
G You always write about history or real people.
H You just tell facts and don't have to worry about a story.
J You can use rhyme to make things sound more important.

© Pearson Education, Inc., publishing as Pearson Prentice Hall. All rights reserved.

Name ______________________________ Date ____________________

Directions: Read the following passages. Then answer the questions. On the answer sheet, fill in the bubble for the answer that you think is correct.

Daniel Parsons lives just four blocks from the hospital. Neighbors call him "Doc" and often stop to visit the retired doctor. Doc was a great doctor because he truly cared about people. When he first retired, he missed his patients. So he moved a big comfortable chair to his front porch, and he sits there when the weather permits. Doc visits with the people who pass by. Many of them are his former patients.

19 According to the story, being a good doctor means —

- **A** living near the hospital
- **B** having a caring personality
- **C** getting plenty of fresh air
- **D** enjoying many houseguests

20 Why does Daniel Parsons visit with former patients?

- **F** He feels obligated.
- **G** He misses them.
- **H** He has nothing better to do.
- **J** none of the above

Directions: Read each sentence. Choose the correct meaning of the underlined word. On the answer sheet, fill in the bubble for the answer that you think is correct.

21 Most people described Paul's personality as being <u>rough</u>.

- **A** uneven
- **B** approximate
- **C** stormy
- **D** harsh

22 Many of us had learned to be cautious in dealing with representatives of the <u>press</u>.

- **F** push against
- **G** news media
- **H** a large machine
- **J** move forward

Directions: Find the meaning of each sentence. On the answer sheet, fill in the bubble for the answer that you think is correct.

23 All hands on deck!

- **A** a card player's demand
- **B** a request for help
- **C** an order to hold onto safety railing
- **D** a command to people to show their palms

24 All the world's a stage, / And all the men and women merely players.

- **F** Live your life while you have the chance.
- **G** In real life, everybody has a part to play.
- **H** Drama gives us insight into the purpose of life.
- **J** Do not be too serious about life's meaning.

© Pearson Education, Inc., publishing as Pearson Prentice Hall. All rights reserved.

Name ______________________________ Date ______________

Directions: Read the following phrases. Then decide which of the four answers has most nearly the same meaning as the underlined word. Then fill in the bubble for the answer that you think is correct.

25 A <u>jaunt</u> in the park
- **A** game
- **B** parade
- **C** pony ride
- **D** short trip

26 A <u>massive</u> building
- **F** large
- **G** brick
- **H** empty
- **J** important

Directions: Read the following words. Look for mistakes in spelling. For each item on the answer sheet, fill in the bubble for the answer that has the mistake. If there is no mistake, fill in the last answer choice.

27
- **A** argue
- **B** vauge
- **C** bounty
- **D** *(No mistakes)*

28
- **F** drums
- **G** music
- **H** radeo
- **J** *(No mistakes)*

Directions: Read the following sentences. Look for mistakes in punctuation. For each item on the answer sheet, fill in the bubble for the answer that has the mistake. If there is no mistake, fill in the last answer choice.

29
- **A** Following the Civil War, Congress passed
- **B** many laws protecting the rights of African
- **C** Americans. Most of them werent followed.
- **D** *(No mistakes)*

30
- **F** Born in San Francisco California
- **G** Russell Freedman published his
- **H** first book in 1961.
- **J** *(No mistakes)*

© Pearson Education, Inc., publishing as Pearson Prentice Hall. All rights reserved.

Name ______________________________ Date ______________

20. Which of the following *best* describes the points of view in *Lesson Plan* and *The Return*?
 A. *Lesson Plan* is in first person; *The Return* is in third person.
 B. *Lesson Plan* is in third person; *The Return* is in first person.
 C. *Lesson Plan* is in second person; *The Return* is in third person.
 D. *Lesson Plan* is in first person; *The Return* is in second person.

21. Why does the poet repeat the word *knock* so often in these lines of poetry?
 What was the constant knock,
 knock, knocking
 Waking me before dawn?
 A. to show that the speaker is expecting a visitor
 B. to show that the speaker has been asleep
 C. to show that there is no doorbell
 D. to show that the knocking is continuous

First Trip

I was happy to be taking my first cross-country trip with my cousin, Beth. As the hours passed, we covered hundreds of miles. The states passed by one after the other, and at the end of the week, we stood on the shore of an ocean that neither of us had ever seen before.

Freedom

Freedom rode in the car with my cousin Beth and me as we painted a bright red line across the map of our country. After many moons, we stood at a new coast.

22. How are the two passages above ***similar***?
 A. Both describe road maps.
 B. Both describe an airplane flight taken by the narrator and Beth.
 C. Both describe a long trip by car.
 D. Both describe the items packed by the narrator and Beth.

23. How are the two passages above ***different***?
 A. They tell two different stories.
 B. *First Trip* has two characters, and *Freedom* has three.
 C. *Freedom* has more metaphors.
 D. *First Trip* is told in first person, and *Freedom* is not.

Read each of the sentences that follow. Then choose the word that ***best*** *expresses the meaning of the underlined word.*

24. The forks and spoons <u>cascaded</u> to the floor.
 A. broke into pieces C. rushed
 B. slid across D. fell like water

25. The <u>nimble</u> mouse evaded the cat's claws.
 A. hungry C. tame
 B. quick D. naughty

© Pearson Education, Inc., publishing as Pearson Prentice Hall. All rights reserved.

Name ______________________ Date ______________

Practice Test 2

Read the following passages. Then answer the questions that follow.

Better Morning

Waking up to a fresh cup of coffee has never been so easy. Percolite Plus offers an auto timer feature that allows you to prepare your coffee the night before. Just pour in the water, fill the filter with coffee, and set the timer. The next morning, the aroma of fresh coffee will awaken you. Percolite Plus is your answer to waking up happy.

Instructions for Percolite Plus Coffeemaker

1. Fill the coffee pot with the desired amount of water (using the numbers on the pot as a guide) by pouring the water into the chamber at the top of the coffeemaker.
2. Place a small filter in the basket at the top of the coffeemaker.
3. Measure the desired amount of ground coffee and place in the filter.
4. Set the timer, if using the auto timer feature.
5. Move switch to ON or AUTO.

1. What is the purpose of the passage *Better Morning*?

A. to sell a product
B. to explain a process
C. to state a fact
D. to make an agreement

2. What does *Instructions for Percolite Plus Coffeemaker* explain?

A. what to do if the coffeemaker breaks
B. why the coffeemaker is a good product
C. when the coffeemaker can be fixed
D. how to operate the coffeemaker

3. From the information in *Better Morning*, what you can conclude about its author?

A. The author wants the details to persuade you to use the coffeemaker.
B. The author is someone who knows a lot about coffee.
C. The author knows how you can have a happier morning.
D. The author drinks coffee every morning.

The Truth About *The Wizard Walks*

Recently, some parents tried to remove *The Wizard Walks* from the shelves of the local public library. These foolish people are entitled to decide for themselves what they will read, but *The Wizard Walks* should not be banned.

The people who object to *The Wizard Walks* believe that it is unsuitable for children. However, a poll showed that most people who want to ban *The Wizard Walks* haven't even read the book. They are mindlessly repeating what they have heard from others without taking the trouble to research the subject themselves.

© Pearson Education, Inc., publishing as Pearson Prentice Hall. All rights reserved.

Name ______________________________ Date ______________

The main argument for banning *The Wizard Walks* is that it is almost a textbook on magic. But anyone who has actually read the book knows that it does not teach witchcraft. Although the main character of *The Wizard Walks* has magical powers, the story is obviously fictional. Most children have no trouble figuring out that this book describes an imaginary world.

Perhaps *The Wizard Walks* is not good for every child, but banning it from the public library goes too far. If ignorant people start banning books, soon our libraries will be empty. Every book is offensive to someone for some reason.

Parents who do not want children to read *The Wizard Walks* can ban it from their homes. To ban it from the public library would take away the right of other parents to make that decision for their own children.

4. Why is the author offended by the attempt to ban *The Wizard Walks*?
   - A. Many supporters of the ban have not read the book.
   - B. The author used *The Wizard Walks* to learn witchcraft.
   - C. The author enjoyed reading *The Wizard Walks* very much.
   - D. Supporters of the ban are prejudiced against witchcraft.

5. Which of these is the *first* clue that the author does not respect the supporters of the ban?
   - A. The author calls the supporters "foolish people."
   - B. The author says the supporters are acting "mindlessly."
   - C. The author says the book is "not good" for all children.
   - D. The author suggests that parents "ban [the book] from their homes."

6. Based on the evidence in this essay, what can you infer that the author believes?
   - A. Only a few books should ever be banned from the library.
   - B. All children should be required to read *The Wizard Walks*.
   - C. *The Wizard Walks* is the best children's book of our time.
   - D. Public libraries should have a wide variety of books.

7. How does the author of the passage make the argument effective?
   - A. The author says negative things about the people who ban books.
   - B. The author states the issues, gives examples, and presents a solution.
   - C. The author agrees that the book may not be good for every child.
   - D. The author says that those who ban books are wrong.

Using Your Chef's Gourmet Hand Mixer

Before using your mixer for the first time, wash and dry the beaters and the mixing bowl. Make sure that the speed control is in the OFF position and the mixer is not plugged in. Insert the beaters into the openings on the bottom of the mixer. Push until each beater clicks into position. Then plug the cord into a standard household electrical outlet (120 volt, 60 Hz A.C.).

8. What should you do just before inserting the beaters?
   - A. Plug the mixer into an outlet.
   - B. Check that the mixer is turned off and unplugged.
   - C. Set the speed control to "1."
   - D. Rock the mixer back onto its base.

© Pearson Education, Inc., publishing as Pearson Prentice Hall. All rights reserved.

Name ______________________________ Date ______________

9. What should you do before using the mixer for the first time?
   A. Wash and dry the beaters and mixing bowl.
   B. Wash and dry the electrical outlet.
   C. Wash and dry the cord.
   D. Wash and dry the speed control.

10. Which of the following is the ***best*** explanation of the purpose of this passage?
   A. The passage describes how to buy The Chef's Gourmet Hand Mixer.
   B. The passage informs how to use The Chef's Gourmet Hand Mixer.
   C. The passage informs how to plug in The Chef's Gourmet Hand Mixer.
   D. The passage describes how to wash The Chef's Gourmet Hand Mixer.

11. Based on the information in this passage, what you can conclude?
   A. The mixer should be operated without the beaters.
   B. The mixer should be operated by professional chefs.
   C. The mixer should be operated near an electrical outlet.
   D. The mixer should be operated outdoors.

Lake Louise

Lake Louise is part of Banff National Park in southern Alberta, Canada. The lake is about a mile and a half long and a third of a mile wide. Visitors find it quiet and peaceful at Lake Louise. The smooth waters mirror the surrounding mountains, creating breathtaking views. More people visit Lake Louise than anywhere else in the Canadian Rockies.

12. Suppose you are writing an essay persuading people to visit Lake Louise. Which of the following statements would be ***most*** effective?
   A. Lake Louise is part of Banff National Park in southern Alberta, Canada.
   B. The lake is about a mile and a half long and a third of a mile wide.
   C. The smooth waters mirror the surrounding mountains, creating breathtaking views.
   D. More people visit Lake Louise than anywhere else in the Canadian Rockies.

13. Which of these statements can be inferred from the paragraph?
   A. Lake Louise is close to the United States.
   B. People enjoy the spectacular scenery at Lake Louise.
   C. Lake Louise is the largest lake in Canada.
   D. The Canadian Rockies have many beautiful lakes.

Modern Bandage

Although many people don't even know his name, Earle Dickson was responsible for creating one of today's most common household items. Dickson was the genius behind Band-Aids®.

In 1917, Dickson was a newly married man and a cotton buyer for a successful bandage company in New Jersey called Johnson & Johnson.

As the story goes, Dickson's wife, Frances, was accident-prone. She often cut herself or nicked her fingers doing various household tasks. The regular bandages were too big and clumsy for Frances, so Dickson devised something better.

© Pearson Education, Inc., publishing as Pearson Prentice Hall. All rights reserved.

He folded pads of cotton gauze and placed them on long strips of surgical tape. He covered this with a material called crinoline. This prevented the tape from sticking to itself when it was rolled back together. Frances could unroll the bandage and cut off as much as she needed.

One day, Dickson mentioned his creation to a friend at work. Soon, Dickson was before the Johnsons, showing them what he had come up with. The Johnsons were especially impressed with the fact that you could put the new bandage on yourself. Up until that point, bandages had been difficult to apply without help.

Johnson & Johnson began producing Band-Aids®, but the bandages didn't take off until the mid-1920s when the company gave thousands of samples to the Boy Scouts. After that, Band-Aids® were a hit. Dickson was made vice president of Johnson & Johnson, and when he died in 1961, the company was selling $30,000,000 dollars' worth of Band-Aids® a year.

14. Here is a partial outline of the passage.

The Invention of Band-Aids®

I. Who Earle Dickson was
II. ______________
III. How Dickson made his own bandage
IV. What happened at Johnson & Johnson
V. The success of Band-Aids®

15. Which answer would fit ***best*** in the blank in the outline?

A. Where Johnson & Johnson was
B. What Dickson's wife's name was
C. Why Dickson made his own bandage
D. How Dickson met with Johnson & Johnson

16. If you were taking notes about this passage, which of these ideas should you ***omit***?

A. Dickson became vice president.
B. Band-Aids® were popular right away.
C. Early bandages were difficult to put on.
D. Dickson worked for Johnson & Johnson.

17. Which of these statements gives the ***best*** summary of the passage?

A. The Boy Scouts make Band-Aids® more popular.
B. A housewife is finally able to bandage herself.
C. A cotton inventor becomes head of a company.
D. One man's homemade bandages become Band-Aids®.

The Growing Popularity of Tennis

The sport of tennis is becoming more popular with children and teenagers.

Part 1

© Pearson Education, Inc., publishing as Pearson Prentice Hall. All rights reserved.

Name ______________________ Date ______________

Young stars such as Andy Roddick and Serena Williams to look up to. Many schools are adding tennis.

Part 2

To their physical education programs. Community centers have recognized the growing popularity of tennis.

Part 3

Added tennis courts to their existing facilities.

18. If you were assigned to write a research report based on information from the passage, what would be the ***best*** information or vocabulary to include?
   A. community centers
   B. growing popularity of tennis
   C. physical education programs
   D. existing facilities

19. Which is the ***best*** way to revise Part 1?
   A. The sport of tennis is becoming more popular with children and teenagers; young stars such as Andy Roddick and Serena Williams to look up to.
   B. With young stars such as Andy Roddick and Serena Williams to look up to, the sport of tennis is becoming more popular with children and teenagers.
   C. Young stars such as Andy Roddick and Serena Williams have made the sport of tennis more popular with children and teenagers.
   D. Young stars such as Andy Roddick and Serena Williams. Have made the sport of tennis more popular with children and teenagers.

20. Suppose that the writer wanted to use the material in this passage to write two paragraphs, with Part 2 appearing at the beginning of the second paragraph. Which of the following would be the *best* transition to the second paragraph?
   A. For instance,
   B. After all,
   C. As a result,
   D. On the contrary,

21. If you were typing this paragraph into a computer's word-processing program, which of the following would be helpful?
   A. The computer can automatically add additional research for you.
   B. You can make corrections easily.
   C. You can move text around easily.
   D. both B and C

Answer the following question.

22. In the sentence, "Maria read many books," which of the following words is the direct object?
   A. Maria
   B. read
   C. many
   D. books

© Pearson Education, Inc., publishing as Pearson Prentice Hall. All rights reserved.

Name ______________________________ Date ______________

Read the following passages. Then answer the questions that follow.

Techniques of Fiction Writers

Fiction writers use a variety of techniques to ______1______ their characters seem like real people. One such technique is to have characters use dialects when they speak. Some writers use first-person narration so that the reader knows how one of the characters feels, as well as what ______2______ says.

23. Suppose you were to make a web showing the sentence that contains the main idea in the center and the sentences that contain details in circles that connect to the center. Which sentence would you place in the center?
    - A. Fiction writers use a variety of techniques to ______1______ their characters seem like real people.
    - B. One such technique is to have characters use dialects when they speak.
    - C. Some writers use first-person narration so that the reader knows how one of the characters feels, as well as what _____2_____ says.
    - D. This paragraph does not contain a main idea.

24. Which of the following words belongs in space 1 as shown in question 22 above?
    - A. makes
    - B. made
    - C. make
    - D. making

25. Which word or group of words belongs in space 2 as shown in question 22 above?
    - A. he or she
    - B. they
    - C. the narrator
    - D. the author

The newspapers in my town and your city ______________ the championship games.

26. Which word or group of words belongs in the space shown in the sentence above?
    - A. covers
    - B. covering
    - C. cover
    - D. has covered

Museum Visit

When we went to the museum, we didn't expect to have a very good time. It was crowded, and my brother said to me, "Do you want me to tell Dad that I'm sick?" I'm glad that I said "no," because within five minutes, we ***are*** interested in what we saw.

27. Which of the following verbs correctly replaces the italicized, boldfaced verb in the passage above?
    - A. was
    - B. were
    - C. had been
    - D. was being

Of the two O'Connor brothers, Chris is the ______________.

28. Which word or group of words belongs in the space shown in the sentence above?
    - A. most athletic
    - B. athletic
    - C. athleticest
    - D. more athletic

© Pearson Education, Inc., publishing as Pearson Prentice Hall. All rights reserved.

Name ______________________________ Date ______________

Carolyn is the sophomore who has the __________ grade point average.

29. Which word or group of words belongs in the space shown in the sentence above?

A. higher
B. highest
C. high
D. more high

Devon failed to pass the lifeguard test the first time __________ therefore, he studied harder before his second attempt.

30. Which mark of punctuation belongs in the space shown in the sentence above?

A. semi-colon
B. exclamation mark
C. period
D. colon

Writing Prompt #1

Imagine that the community center in your town will soon be adding something new. What do you think should be added? It may be a new piece of equipment, a new club, or a new class that you would like to take. It might be something you can use or take part in after school, on weekends, or during summer vacation. Write to convince the director of the community center that your idea is the one that should be added. Be sure to be specific and explain your reasons.

Writing Prompt #2

If you had three wishes, what you wish for and why? Think about your three wishes and why you chose them. Perhaps your wishes have to do with a place or an event that you remember from your past. Maybe your wishes would make you and/or other people happy. You might think also about how the wishes could help change the world for the better. Write an essay in which you explain what you wish for and why. Support your ideas with examples and details.

© Pearson Education, Inc., publishing as Pearson Prentice Hall. All rights reserved.

Name ______________________ Date ______________

Practice Test 3

Part 1: Textual Analysis

Read the following narrative and then answer the questions that follow.

from *The Pioneers* by James Fenimore Cooper

James Fenimore Cooper wrote action-filled adventure stories that were very popular. The central character in five of his novels is a wilderness hunter named Natty Bumppo, or Leather-stocking, who lives between the Indian and white worlds. Bumppo has learned the forest skills of the Indians. This selection is from The Pioneers. In this scene, Leather- stocking realizes that the wilderness is fast falling to settlers.

1) The heavens were alive with pigeons; the whole village seemed equally in motion, with men, women, and children. Every species of fire - arms, from the French ducking-gun, with a barrel near six feet in length, to the common horseman's pistol, was to be seen in the hands of the men and boys; while bows and arrows, some made of the simple stick of a walnut sapling, and others in a rude [simple] imitation of the ancient cross-bows, were carried by many of the latter. . . .

2) Amongst the sportsmen was the tall, gaunt form of Leather-stocking, walking over the field, with his rifle hanging on his arm, his dogs at his heels; the latter now scenting the dead or wounded birds, that were beginning to tumble from the flocks, and then crouching under the legs of their master, as if they participated in his feelings, at this wasteful and unsportsmanlike execution.

3) The reports of the fire-arms became rapid, whole volleys rising from the plain, as flocks of more than ordinary numbers darted over the opening, shadowing the field, like a cloud; and then the light smoke of a single piece would issue from among the leafless bushes on the mountain, as death was hurled on the retreat of the affrighted birds, who were rising from a volley, in a vain effort to escape.

4) Arrows, and missiles of every kind, were in the midst of the flocks; and so numerous were the bird s , and so low did they take their flight, that even long poles, in the hands of those on the sides of the mountain, were used to strike them to the earth. . . .So prodigious was the number of birds, that the scattering fire of the guns, with the hurling of missiles, and the cries of the boys, had no other effect than to break off small flocks from the immense masses that continued to dart along the valley, as if the whole of the feathered tribe were pouring through one pass.

5) None pretended to collect the game, which lay scattered over the fields in such profusion, as to cover the very ground with the fluttering victims. Leather-stocking was a silent, but uneasy spectator of all these proceedings, but was able to keep his sentiments to himself until he saw the introduction of the swivel [cannon] into the sports.

6) "This comes of settling a country!" he said — " here have I known the pigeons to fly for forty long years, and, till you made your clearings, there was nobody to skear [scare]or to hurt them. I loved to see them come into the woods, for they were company to a body; hurting nothing; being, as it was, as harmless as a garter-snake. But now it gives me sore thoughts when I hear the frighty things whizzing through the air, for I know it's only a motion to bring out all the brats in the village. Well! the Lord won't see the waste of his creators for nothing, and right will be done to the pigeons, as well as others, by-and-by. . . .

© Pearson Education, Inc., publishing as Pearson Prentice Hall. All rights reserved.

Name ______________________________ Date ______________

7) " Among the sportsmen was Billy Kirby, who, armed with an old musket, was loading, and, without even looking into the air, was firing, and shouting as his victims fell even on his own person. He heard the speech of Natty, and took upon himself to reply "What! old Leather-stocking," he cried, "grumbling at the loss of a few pigeons! If you had to sow your wheat twice, and three times, as I have done, you wouldn't be so massy-fully [mercifully] feeling'd to'wards the divils.—Hurrah, boys! scatter the feathers. This is better than shooting at a turkey's head and neck, old fellow."

8) "It's better for you, maybe, Billy Kirby," replied the indignant old hunter, "and all them that don't know how to put a ball down a rifle-barrel, or how to bring it up ag'in with a true aim; but it's wicked to be shooting into flocks in this wastey manner; and none do it, who know how to knock over a single bird. If a body has a craving for pigeon's flesh, why! it's made the same as all other creator's, for man's eating, but not to kill twenty and eat one."

© Pearson Education, Inc., publishing as Pearson Prentice Hall. All rights reserved.

Name ______________________ Date ______________

1 **Which of the following best describes Leather Stocking?**

- **A** pioneer clothing
- **B** an old Indian
- **C** a wilderness hunter
- **D** a young farmer

2 **What is the main idea of the selection?**

- **A** Leather Stocking does not like the pioneers.
- **B** Leather Stocking thinks you should never kill pigeons.
- **C** Leather Stocking does not believe wildlife should be killed for sport.
- **D** Leather Stocking does not like guns.

3 **Which of the following best describes Billy Kirby?**

- **A** A pioneer that does not like Leather Stocking.
- **B** A farmer who thinks he is protecting his crops.
- **C** A pioneer who thinks it is fun to kill the pigeons.
- **D** A farmer who wants to show off for his friends.

4 **Why most likely did the author use the word "skear" instead of scare?**

- **A** He did not know the correct spelling.
- **B** He likes to write dialogue.
- **C** He is showing Leather Stocking's dialect.
- **D** He is showing how the word was written in pioneer days.

5 **How *most likely* did Natty Bumppo get the name Leather Stocking?**

- **A** because of his clothing
- **B** because he lived with the Indians
- **C** because he wanted to change his name
- **D** because the pioneers did not like him.

6 **Which of the following relationships is most similar to the relationship below?**

Leather Stocking : pigeons

- **A** Indians :pioneers
- **B** Pioneers : Indians
- **C** Billy Kirby :crops
- **D** Crops : Billy Kirby

7 **Which of the following best describes the conflict in the selection?**

- **A** man verses man
- **B** wildlife verses wilderness
- **C** nature verses wilderness
- **D** man verses environment

8 **Based on paragraph 4, what is the meaning of the word *prodigious*?**

- **A** birds
- **B** angry
- **C** enormous
- **D** weak

9 **Based on paragraph 8, what is the meaning of *indignant*?**

- **A** uneasy
- **B** unfair
- **C** anxious
- **D** angry

10 **Which of the following best fits the Venn diagram?**

Leather Stocking	Bill Kirby
Hunter	farmer
Old	young
Lives in the woods	lives in a community

- **A** gaunt
- **B** sportsman
- **C** pioneer
- **D** lonely

© Pearson Education, Inc., publishing as Pearson Prentice Hall. All rights reserved.

Name ______________________ Date ______________

Jabberwocky by Lewis Carroll

"Jabberwocky" is generally considered the greatest of all nonsense poems. It can be found in the first chapter of Through the looking Glass and What Alice Found There. You may know_this novel better as_ Alice in Wonderland. The following quote follows the poem in the novel:

"It sees very pretty," she said when she had finished it, "but it's rather hard to understand!" (You see she didn't like to confess even to herself, that she couldn't make it out at all.)

Humpty Dumpty explained some of the words. Read the following definitions and answer the questions after the poem.

Brillig : 4:00pm, the time to cook dinner

Slithy: Smooth and active

Tove: something like a bagger_ something like a lizard

Gyre: to go round and around

Gimble: to make holes

Wabe : a grass plot beside a sundial

Mimsy : flimsy and miserable

Borogove: a shabby looking bird

Mome raths : lost green pigs

Outgrabe : something between bellowing and whistling with a sneeze in the middle.

'Twas brillig, and the slithy toves
Did gyre and gimble in the wabe;
All mimsy were the borogoves,
And the mome raths outgrabe.

"Beware the Jabberwock, my son!
The jaws that bite, the claws that catch!
Beware the Jubjub bird, and shun
The frumious Bandersnatch!"

He took his vorpal sword in hand:
Long time the manxome foe he sought--
So rested he by the Tumtum tree,
And stood awhile in thought.

And, as in uffish thought he stood,
The Jabberwock, with eyes of flame,
Came whiffling through the tulgey wood,
And burbled as it came!

One two! One two! And through and through
The vorpal blade went snicker-snack!
He left it dead, and with its head
He went galumphing back.

© Pearson Education, Inc., publishing as Pearson Prentice Hall. All rights reserved.

Name ______________________ Date ______________

"And hast thou slain the Jabberwock?
Come to my arms, my beamish boy!
O frabjous day! Callooh! Callay!"
He chortled in his joy.

'Twas brillig, and the slithy toves
Did gyre and gimble in the wabe;
All mimsy were the borogoves,
And the mome raths outgrabe.

11 What *most likely* is the Jabberwock?

A a person

B a creature

C a type of food

D a kind of bird

12 Which of the following would be *most* like Alice's experience in the selection?

A being given asked to read a very difficult book.

B being asked to read a book in a foreign language

C talking to an imaginary character

D reading a fantasy novel

13 Which of the following is *most likely* the meaning of frabjous in stanza 6?

A fabulous

B wonderful and beautiful

C fabulous and joyous

D joyous

14 Which is the *best* restatement of stanzas 1 and 7?

A I was cooking troves for dinner and listening to the green pigs as they cried for help.

B I was cooking dinner, the troves were making holes in the grass and the green pigs were making noises.

C I was looking for something to cook for dinner when I saw the monster.

D I was cooking dinner when I heard strange noises coming from the woods.

15 What most likely is the meaning of *manxome* in stanza 3?

A large and fierce

B small and strong

C mythical and loud

D unusual and silent

16 What is the author's tone?

A serious

B ironic

C sarcastic

D humorous

17 Which of the following is *most similar* to the selection?

A a science fiction poem

B a poem about slaying a dragon

C a poem about the Renaissance

D a realistic poem

© Pearson Education, Inc., publishing as Pearson Prentice Hall. All rights reserved.

Name ______________________________ Date ______________

Fine Art: Remembering the work of Maya Ying Lin

1) Maya Lin competed with over 1,400 other entrants to design the Vietnam Veterans Memorial. When the board of directors of the Southern Poverty Law Center (SPLC) in Montgomery, Alabama decided they wanted a civil rights memorial, they called every Lin in the New York City phone book looking for Maya. They knew exactly who they wanted to design their memorial.

2) The SPLC was founded in 1971 to protect and advance the legal rights of minorities and poor people, and it remains one of the nation's leading civil rights organizations.

3) Maya, inspired by the historical significance of the civil rights movement, agreed to design the monument. In researching the background of the civil rights movement, she came across these words by Martin Luther King, Jr.:

"We will not be satisfied until justice rolls down like waters, and righteousness like a mighty stream."

4) King used these words from the Bible in several of his speeches. The words inspired Maya to use water as a main design element of the monument. The plan was to memorialize those individuals who had been killed in the cause of marching for civil rights.

5) The SPLC came up with 53 entries they wanted etched in stone. Maya decided to create a huge, twelve-foot disk, or table of granite and to inscribe the names around the perimeter. The entries would be listed in chronological order from 17 May 1954, the Supreme Court ruling outlawing school segregation, to 4 April 1968, the assassination of Martin Luther King, Jr.

6) A black granite wall behind the disk rising nine feet would be inscribed with the words that inspired Maya, *"until justice rolls down like waters, and righteousness like a mighty stream."* Water would flow down the wall and across the disk, touching each name in the timeline. The disk would be close to the ground so people could walk around it and touch the inscriptions.

18 **Why *most likely* did the SPLC know they wanted Maya Lin to create their memorial?**

- **A** They like oriental art.
- **B** They liked her other work.
- **C** They knew where she lived.
- **D** They wanted someone famous.

19 **Why was the SPLC founded?**

- **A** to become civil rights organization.
- **B** to honor Martin Luther King
- **C** to protect the legal rights of the poor and minorities.
- **D** to research and protect civil rights.

20 **What is the meaning of the figurative language in Paragraph 3?**

- **A** We will not stop until there is justice for everyone.
- **B** We will roll down the river until it stops.
- **C** We will not let the water stop us.
- **D** We will not be satisfied with current civil rights.

21 **Why most likely did Lin use water in her monument?**

- **A** It symbolized Civil Rights.
- **B** It was restful to watch
- **C** It symbolized King's determination.
- **D** It was what the SPLC asked her to do.

© Pearson Education, Inc., publishing as Pearson Prentice Hall. All rights reserved.

Name ______________________________ Date ______________

How I became a Printer By Benjamin Franklin

This excerpt from Benjamin Franklin's autobiography describes his early education and his apprenticeship to his brother James, a Boston printer. Franklin also writes about the role printers played in bringing attention to colonial opposition to British rule.

From Social Studies © Prentice-Hall, Inc.

1) I was put to the grammar-school at eight years of age, my father intending to devote me, as the tithe of his sons, to the service of the Church. My early readiness in learning to read (which must have been very early, as I do not remember when I could not read), and the opinion of all his friends, that I should certainly make a good scholar, encouraged him in this purpose of his.

2) But my father, in the mean time, from the view of the expense of a college education, which having so large a family he could not well afford . . . took me from the grammar-school, and sent me to a school for writing and arithmetic. . . . At ten years old, I was taken home to assist my father in his business, which was that of a tallow-chandler and soap boiler. . . .

3) Accordingly, I was employed in cutting wick for the candles, filling the dipping mold and the molds for cast candles, attending the shop, going of errands etc.

4) I disliked the trade, and had a strong inclination for the sea, but my father declared against it. However, living near the water, I was much in and about it, learned early to swim well, and to manage boats; and when in a boat or canoe with other boys, I was commonly allowed to govern, especially in any case of difficulty; and upon other occasions I was generally a leader among the boys. . . .

5) From a child I was fond of reading, and all the little money that came into my hands was ever laid out in books. . . . This bookish inclination at length determined my father to make me a printer, though he had already one son (James) of that profession.

6) In 1717 my brother James returned from England with a press and letters to set up his business in Boston. I liked it much better than that of my father, but still had a hankering for the sea. To prevent the apprehended effect of such an inclination, my father was impatient to have me bound to my brother. I stood out some time, but at last was persuaded, and signed the indenture when I was yet but twelve years old. I was to serve as an apprentice till I was twenty-one years of age, only I was to be allowed journeyman's wages during the last year.

7) In a little time I made great proficiency in the business, and became a useful hand to my brother. Though as brother, he considered himself as my master, and me as his apprentice, and accordingly, expected the same services from me as he would from another, while I thought he demeaned me too much in some he required of me, who from a brother expected more indulgence.

8) Our disputes were often brought before our father, and I fancy I was either generally in the right, or else a better pleader, because the judgment was generally in my favor. But my brother was passionate, and had often beaten me, which I took extremely amiss; and, thinking my apprenticeship very tedious, I was continually wishing for some opportunity of shortening it, which at length offered in a manner unexpected.

9) One of the pieces in our newspaper on some political point, which I have now forgotten, gave offense to the Assembly. He [James] was taken up, censured, and imprisoned for a month, by the speaker's warrant, I suppose, because he would not discover [reveal] his author. I too was taken up and examined before the council; but, though I did not give them any satisfaction, they contented themselves with admonishing me, and dismissed me, considering me, perhaps, as an apprentice, who was bound to keep his master's secrets.

© Pearson Education, Inc., publishing as Pearson Prentice Hall. All rights reserved.

Name ______________________________ Date ______________

10) During my brother's confinement, which I resented a good deal, not withstanding our private differences, I had the management of the paper; and I made bold to give our rulers some rubs in it, which my brother took very kindly, while others began to consider me in an unfavorable light, as a young genius that had a turn for libeling and satire. My brother's discharge was accompanied with an order of the House (a very odd one), that "James Franklin should no longer print the paper called the New England Courant."

11) There was a consultation held in our printing-house among his friends, what he should do in this case. Some proposed to evade the order by changing the name of the paper; but my brother, seeing inconveniences in that, it was finally concluded on as a better way, to let it be printed for the future under the name of BENJAMIN FRANKLIN; and to avoid the censure of the Assembly, that might fall on him as still printing it by his apprentice, the contrivance was that my old indenture should be returned to me, with full discharge on the back of it, to be shown on occasion, but to secure to him the benefit of my service, I was to sign new indentures for the remainder of the term, which were to be kept private. A very flimsy scheme it was; however, it was immediately executed, and the paper went on accordingly, under my name for several months.

© Pearson Education, Inc., publishing as Pearson Prentice Hall. All rights reserved.

Name ______________________ Date ______________

22 **Why *most likely* did Benjamin's father send him to school?**

A He wanted one of his children to be educated.

B He wanted his son to help him in his business.

C He wanted Benjamin to become famous.

D He believed that Benjamin was smart.

23 **What is the meaning of *govern* in paragraph 4?**

A swim

B row

C control

D trade

24 **Why did Benjamin's father want him to go to work with his brother?**

A to keep him from becoming a sailor.

B to keep him working for the family.

C because his brother needed help.

D because his brother wanted an indentured servant.

25 **Why *most likely* did Benjamin resent his brother imprisonment?**

A It made his work harder.

B He believed in free speech.

C He wanted to run the paper

D It made their father mad.

26 **Why was the name of the paper changed to BENJAMIN FRANKLIN?**

A Benjamin named the new paper after himself.

B Benjamin bought the paper from his brother.

C The government would not let James continue to print his paper.

D The government made James change the name of his paper.

27 **Why did James release Benjamin from his indenture?**

A because he had helped him.

B because he wanted to trick the government.

C because his father asked for Franklin's freedom.

D Because his time was up

28 **What is the meaning of *admonishing* in paragraph 9?**

A imprisoning

B dismissing

C managing

D warning

29 **How were Benjamin and James similar?**

A They both owned newspapers.

B They were both put in jail.

C They both wanted to be sailors.

D They both liked to write.

30 **Why most likely did Benjamin think he was right when he and his brother had a dispute.**

A His brother always gave in.

B His father liked him best.

C His brother had gone to jail.

D His father usually agreed with him

© Pearson Education, Inc., publishing as Pearson Prentice Hall. All rights reserved.

Name ______________________________ Date ______________

Drama Critical Reading

Read both parts of the selection and answer the following questions based on their content and on the relationship between them.

Part 1

It is springtime and a young girl, Melinda, is in the garden in front of the small cottage where she lives with her mother who is a widow. There are beautiful flowers all around. Melinda is tended the flowers as her mother enters the stage.

from *The Girl Whose Fortune Sought Her* by Patricia Clapp

Characters

MELINDA WIDOW CLOWN PEDDLER GIRL MAN

WIDOW: That's right, be gentle with them. Careful of those new little leaves.

MELINDA: Yes, Mother.

WIDOW: We must be gentle with all living things, Melinda, whether they're plants or people.

MELINDA: Yes, Mother.

WIDOW: You have a nice touch with flowers, child.

MELINDA: Thank you, Mother.

WIDOW: What's the matter, child? You don't seem happy. Is something wrong?

MELINDA: No, Mother.

WIDOW: "Yes, Mother; no, Mother; thank you, Mother";—what is it Melinda? It isn't like you to be so quiet. Tell me what the trouble is.

MELINDA *(Suddenly throwing down her towel and shears)*: I'm just tired of staying home all day, day after day, doing nothing but tending the flowers and sweeping the floors and drying the dishes. I want to go away, to find something big to do. Mother, I want to go to seek my fortune!

Part 2

Finn McCool,in Irish legends is a giant.His home is high on Knockmany mountain. When the play begins, UNA is washing clothes outside and the children are sitting nearby in the yard.

from *Finn McCool* by May Lynch

Characters

FINN McCOOL; UNA, his wife; his children: OWEN, JOHN, JAMIE, MEG, CELIA

UNA: There! That's the last of my washing, and I must say it was a big one.

OWEN: I'll say it was. I carried six buckets of water up Knockmany Mountain this morning.

© Pearson Education, Inc., publishing as Pearson Prentice Hall. All rights reserved.

Name ______________________ Date ______________

JOHN: And so did Jamie and I. We do it all the time.

OWEN: You didn't carry six buckets, John.

JAMIE *(Laughing)*: No, Owen, but you spilled half of yours.

OWEN: I did not, Jamie McCool!

JAMIE: You did, too.

OWEN *(Loudly)*: I did not!

UNA: Children! Stop that brawling and squalling. My, I'll be glad when your father, Finn McCool, finds us a spring up here near the house.

JOHN: He says that there's water right out there under those two rocks.

JAMIE: Yes, and he's going to move them someday.

OWEN *(Interrupting)*: Someday! Someday! He keeps saying *someday*, but *someday* never comes.

UNA: Owen McCool, don't speak that way of your father. After all, the dear man is very busy and tired—and—and busy. (MEG *and* CELIA *enter.*)

CELIA: Mother! Mother! Guess what?

MEG: Grannie Owen and Mrs. O'Malley and Mrs. Shane are coming up Knockmany Mountain right now.

© Pearson Education, Inc., publishing as Pearson Prentice Hall. All rights reserved.

Name ______________________ Date ______________

31 **Based on the title of part 1, what do you predict will happen to Melinda?**

A She will move away to seek her fortune.

B She will get a job as a gardener.

C She will stay home and her fortune will find her.

D She will convince her mother to give her different chores.

32 **How are the settings of both dramas similar?**

A They are both in Ireland.

B They are both in springtime.

C They are both in the yard.

D They are both in a family home.

33 **Which of the following is similar to the way Una feels about Finn?**

A showing anger

B being helpful

C being concerned

D showing loneliness

34 **Which of the following best describes Melinda?**

A She is very proud of the flowers.

B She likes to sweep and clean.

C She wants to leave home.

D She is usually very talkative.

35 **What do the stage directions tell the reader about Melinda?**

A She is good with the flowers.

B She is very polite to her mother

C She is frustrated with gardening.

D She wants to leave her mother.

36 **What do both mothers have in common?**

A They both try to help their children with their problems.

B They are both very busy.

C They both want their children to be gentle.

D They both have children to help with chores.

37 **How are Melinda and Owen similar?**

A They are the oldest children.

B They both have complaints about their lives.

C They both give their mothers advice.

D They are both very spoiled.

© Pearson Education, Inc., publishing as Pearson Prentice Hall. All rights reserved.

Name ______________________ Date ______________

Casey at the Bat by Ernest Lawrence Thayer

The outlook wasn't brilliant for the Mudville nine that day:
The score stood four to two, with but one inning more to play,
And then when Cooney died at first, and Barrows did the same,
A pall-like silence fell upon the patrons of the game.

A straggling few got up to go in deep despair. The rest
Clung to that hope which springs eternal in the human breast;
They thought, "If only Casey could but get a whack at that—
We'd put up even money now, with Casey at the bat.

But Flynn preceded Casey, as did also Jimmy Blake,
And the former was a hoodoo, while the latter was a cake;
So upon that stricken multitude grim melancholy sat,
For there seemed but little chance of Casey getting to the bat.

But Flynn let drive a single, to the wonderment of all,
And Blake, the much despised, tore the cover off the ball;
And when the dust had lifted, and men saw what had occurred,
There was Jimmy safe at second and Flynn a-hugging third.

Then from five thousand throats and more there rose a lusty yell;
It rumbled through the valley, it rattled in the dell;
It pounded on the mountain and recoiled upon the flat,
For Casey, mighty Casey, was advancing to the bat.

There was ease in Casey's manner as he stepped into his place;
There was pride in Casey's bearing and a smile lit Casey's face.
And when, responding to the cheers, he lightly doffed his hat,
No stranger in the crowd could doubt 'twas Casey at the bat.

Ten thousand eyes were on him as he rubbed his hands with dirt;
Five thousand tongues applauded when he wiped them on his shirt;
Then while the writhing pitcher ground the ball into his hip,
Defiance flashed in Casey's eye, a sneer curled Casey's lip.

And now the leather-covered sphere came hurtling through the air,
And Casey stood a-watching it in haughty grandeur there.
Close by the sturdy batsman the ball unheeded sped—
"That ain't my style," said Casey. "Strike one!" the umpire said.

From the benches, black with people, there went up a muffled roar, Like the beating of the storm-waves on a stern and distant shore;
"Kill him! Kill the umpire!" shouted someone on the stand;
And it's likely they'd have killed him had not Casey raised his hand.

© Pearson Education, Inc., publishing as Pearson Prentice Hall. All rights reserved.

Name ______________________________ Date ______________

With a smile of Christian charity great Casey's visage shone;
He stilled the rising tumult; he bade the game go on;
He signaled to the pitcher, and once more the dun sphere flew;
But Casey still ignored it and the umpire said, "Strike two!"

"Fraud!" cried the maddened thousands, and echo answered "Fraud!"
But one scornful look from Casey and the audience was awed.
They saw his face grow stern and cold, they saw his muscles strain,
And they knew that Casey wouldn't let that ball go by again.

The sneer is gone from Casey's lip, his teeth are clenched in hate,
He pounds with cruel violence his bat upon the plate;
And now the pitcher holds the ball, and now he lets it go,
And now the air is shattered by the force of Casey's blow.

Oh, somewhere in this favored land the sun is shining bright,
The band is playing somewhere, and somewhere hearts are light;
And somewhere men are laughing, and somewhere children shout,
But there is no joy in Mudville—mighty Casey has struck out.

© Pearson Education, Inc., publishing as Pearson Prentice Hall. All rights reserved.

Name ______________________ Date ______________

38 Why is the selection a narrative poem?

A It has a rhyming beat.

B It is about a person.

C It only has one speaker.

D It tells a story.

39 What is the speaker's opinion of Flynn and Blake in stanza 3?

A He does not want them on the team.

B He thinks they are good players.

C He thinks they are weak players.

D He wants them thrown out of the game.

40 Based on stanza 5, what happened when Casey walked to home plate to bat?

A The crowd became very quiet.

B The crowd yelled wildly.

C People all around the country side started yelling.

D People became very concerned.

41 Which of the following *best* describes Casey

A A good player who never misses the ball.

B The best player on the team.

C A good player who is overly confident.

D The only player who smiles at the crowd.

42 What is ironic about the poem?

A The players that the speaker thought were weak hit the ball and Casey did not.

B The crowd was yelling at the umpire not at the players.

C The very loud crowd became very quiet at the end of the poem.

D The crowd changed from very happy with Casey to very angry with him.

43 Based on the context of stanza 10, what is the meaning of visage?

A baseball term

B umpire's term

C facial expression

D happy expression

44 Why *most likely* did Casey not try to hit the first two balls?

A The balls were no good..

B He was showing off.

C He wanted to frighten the crowd.

D The balls were hard to hit.

45 Why was it important for Casey to hit the ball at the time described in the selection?

A The team was losing badly.

B The team had a chance to make one or possibly two runs.

C It was the last chance for Casey to play with the team.

D It was the last game of the season.

© Pearson Education, Inc., publishing as Pearson Prentice Hall. All rights reserved.

Name ______________________________ Date ______________

Dracula by Bram Stoker 1897 Edition

1) *Fictional stories about vampires have always fascinated readers. You may have read a vampire story or possibly you have seen the movie Buffy the Vampire Slayer or an episode of the television series of the same name. Almost everyone enjoys a good scary story. Read the following excerpt from chapter two of Bram Stoker's Dracula the 1897 edition. Most readers would agree that Dracula is the "Grand-daddy" of the vampire stories.*

CHAPTER 2

Jonathan Harker's Journal Continued

2) 5 May.--I must have been asleep, for certainly if I had been fully awake I must have noticed the approach of such a remarkable place. In the gloom the courtyard looked of considerable size, and as several dark ways led from it under great round arches, it perhaps seemed bigger than it really is. I have not yet been able to see it by daylight.

3) When the caleche stopped, the driver jumped down and held out his hand to assist me to alight. Again I could not but notice his prodigious strength. His hand actually seemed like a steel vice that could have crushed mine if he had chosen. Then he took my traps, and placed them on the ground beside me as I stood close to a great door, old and studded with large iron nails, and set in a projecting doorway of massive stone. I could see even in the dim light that the stone was massively carved, but that the carving had been much worn by time and weather. As I stood, the driver jumped again into his seat and shook the reins. The horses started forward, and trap and all disappeared down one of the dark openings.

4) I stood in silence where I was, for I did not know what to do. Of bell or knocker there was no sign. Through these frowning walls and dark window openings it was not likely that my voice could penetrate. The time I waited seemed endless, and I felt doubts and fears crowding upon me. What sort of place had I come to, and among what kind of people? What sort of grim adventure was it on which I had embarked?....

5) ... I heard a heavy step approaching behind the great door, and saw through the chinks the gleam of a coming light. Then there was the sound of rattling chains and the clanking of massive bolts drawn back. A key was turned with the loud grating noise of long disuse, and the great door swung back.

6) Within, stood a tall old man, clean-shaven save for a long white moustache, and clad in black from head to foot, without a single speck of colour about him anywhere. He held in his hand an antique silver lamp, in which the flame burned without a chimney or globe of any kind, throwing long quivering shadows as it flickered in the draught of the open door. The old man motioned me in with his right hand with a courtly gesture, saying in excellent English, but with a strange intonation.

7) "Welcome to my house! Enter freely and of your own free will!" He made no motion of stepping to meet me, but stood like a statue, as though his gesture of welcome had fixed him into stone. The instant, however, that I had stepped over the threshold, he moved impulsively forward, and holding out his hand grasped mine with a strength which made me wince, an effect which was not lessened by the fact that it seemed cold as ice, more like the hand of a dead than a living man. Again he said,

8) "Welcome to my house! Enter freely. Go safely, and leave something of the happiness you

© Pearson Education, Inc., publishing as Pearson Prentice Hall. All rights reserved.

bring!" The strength of the handshake was so much akin to that which I had noticed in the driver, whose face I had not seen, that for a moment I doubted if it were not the same person to whom I was speaking. So to make sure, I said interrogatively, "Count Dracula?"

9) He bowed in a courtly way as he replied, "I am Dracula, and I bid you welcome, Mr. Harker, to my house. Come in, the night air is chill, and you must need to eat and rest." As he was speaking, he put the lamp on a bracket on the wall, and stepping out, took my luggage. He had carried it in before I could forestall him. I protested, but he insisted.

10) "Nay, sir, you are my guest. It is late, and my people are not available. Let me see to your comfort myself." He insisted on carrying my traps along the passage, and then up a great winding stair, and along another great passage, on whose stone floor our steps rang heavily. At the end of this he threw open a heavy door, and I rejoiced to see within a well-lit room in which a table was spread for supper, and on whose mighty hearth a great fire of logs, freshly replenished, flamed and flared.

11) The Count halted, putting down my bags, closed the door, and crossing the room, opened another door, which led into a small octagonal room lit by a single lamp, and seemingly without a window of any sort. Passing through this, he opened another door, and motioned me to enter. It was a welcome sight. For here was a great bedroom well lighted and warmed with another log fire, also added to but lately, for the top logs were fresh, which sent a hollow roar up the wide chimney. The Count himself left my luggage inside and withdrew, saying, before he closed the door.

12) "You will need, after your journey, to refresh yourself by making your toilet. I trust you will find all you wish. When you are ready, come into the other room, where you will find your supper prepared."

13) The light and warmth and the Count's courteous welcome seemed to have dissipated all my doubts and fears. Having then reached my normal state, I discovered that I was half famished with hunger. So making a hasty toilet, I went into the other room.

14) I found supper already laid out. My host, who stood on one side of the great fireplace, leaning against the stonework, made a graceful wave of his hand to the table, and said, "I pray you, be seated and sup how you please. You will I trust, excuse me that I do not join you, but I have dined already, and I do not sup."

15) The count himself came forward and took off the cover of a dish, and I fell to at once on an excellent roast chicken. This, with some cheese and a salad and a bottle of old tokay, of which I had two glasses, was my supper. During the time I was eating it the Count asked me many questions as to my journey, and I told him by degrees all I had experienced.

16) By this time, I had finished my supper, and by my host's desire had drawn up a chair by the fire and begun to smoke a cigar, which he offered me, at the same time excusing himself that he did not smoke. I had now an opportunity of observing him, and found him of a very marked physiognomy.

17) His face was a strong, a very strong, aquiline, with high bridge of the thin nose and peculiarly arched nostrils, with lofty domed forehead, and hair growing scantily round the temples but profusely elsewhere. His eyebrows were very massive, almost meeting over the nose, and with bushy hair that seemed to curl in its own profusion. The mouth, so far as I could see it under the heavy moustache, was fixed and rather cruel-looking, with peculiarly sharp white teeth. These protruded over the lips, whose remarkable ruddiness showed astonishing vitality in a man of his years. For the rest, his ears were pale, and at the tops extremely pointed. The chin was broad and strong, and the cheeks firm though thin. The general effect was one of extraordinary pallor.

18) Hitherto, I had noticed the backs of his hands as they lay on his knees in the firelight, and they

© Pearson Education, Inc., publishing as Pearson Prentice Hall. All rights reserved.

had seemed rather white and fine. But seeing them now close to me, I could not but notice that they were rather coarse, broad, with squat fingers. Strange to say, there were hairs in the centre of the palm. The nails were long and fine, and cut to a sharp point. As the Count leaned over me and his hands touched me, I could not repress a shudder. It may have been that his breath was rank, but a horrible feeling of nausea came over me, which, do what I would, I could not conceal.

19) The Count, evidently noticing it, drew back. And with a grim sort of smile, which showed more than he had yet done his protuberant teeth, sat himself down again on his own side of the fireplace. We were both silent for a while, and as I looked towards the window I saw the first dim streak of the coming dawn. There seemed a strange stillness over everything. But as I listened, I heard as if from down below in the valley the howling of many wolves. The Count's eyes gleamed, and he said.

20) "Listen to them, the children of the night. What music they make!" Seeing, I suppose, some expression in my face strange to him, he added, "Ah, sir, you dwellers in the city cannot enter into the feelings of the hunter." Then he rose and said.

21) "But you must be tired. Your bedroom is all ready, and tomorrow you shall sleep as late as you will. I have to be away till the afternoon, so sleep well and dream well!" With a courteous bow, he opened for me himself the door to the octagonal room, and I entered my bedroom.

22) I am all in a sea of wonders. I doubt. I fear. I think strange things, which I dare not confess to my own soul. God keep me, if only for the sake of those dear to me!

© Pearson Education, Inc., publishing as Pearson Prentice Hall. All rights reserved.

Name ______________________ Date ______________

46 Based on the context of paragraph 3, what is the meaning of caleche?

A a coachman

B a castle

C a carriage

D a door

47 What did Jonathan find unusual about the Count's behavior in paragraph 7?

A He had very cold hands.

B He moved quickly for an old man.

C He had great strength.

D He did not step to meet his visitor.

48 Which of the following best describes the author's purpose for paragraph 17?

A It lets the reader know how the Count looked.

B It lets the reader know that the Count had bad breath.

C It lets the reader know that the Count seemed friendly.

D It lets the reader know that the Count was very strong.

49 Which best describes the Count's feelings towards the wolves in paragraph 20?

A He appreciates the wolves.

B He fears the wolves.

C He feels the wolves are his children.

D He considers himself a hunter.

50 Which of the following best describe the Count in the selection?

A evil and frightening

B strong and very pale

C cold and talkative

D mysterious and courteous

51 Which of the following best describes how Jonathan reacts to this meeting.

A He is cold and frightened.

B He likes his food and his nice sleeping quarters.

C He is confused and fearful of his own thoughts.

D He doesn't understand what is happening.

52 Which of the following does the author use most often in the selection to create reader interest.

A vivid descriptions

B suspense

C figurative language

D sounds

© Pearson Education, Inc., publishing as Pearson Prentice Hall. All rights reserved.

Name ______________________________ Date ______________

Thank You Letters *are always appreciated*

Has someone done something nice for you recently? Are you planning to look for a summer job? Well, if you answered yes to either of these questions this news is for you.

Many people forget or overlook writing a thank you note. However, they are appropriate, show good manners and are a sincere way to show your interest.

Personal thank you notes should be sent when someone has done something special for you. It could be that they went out of their way to help you with a project or maybe they took time from their busy schedule to take you somewhere. Thank you notes aren't just for presents, but of course, you would want to send a note if you did receive a gift.

Before you begin to write think about the person you are planning to thank. It is always nice to mention something in the note that you have in common. Thank you notes don't have to be long. A short, to the point note that is sincere will have meaning for the person that receives your letter. In this very busy world, a hand written thank you note is a pleasant surprise to find in the mailbox.

A thank you note after a job interview can reap great rewards. Often, this step is overlooked. The note will make your name stand out in the interviewers mind and might help you land a great summer job. The note should be written the day after your interview. Unlike the personal thank you note, the business thank you should be written on your typewriter or computer. The paper should be nice but not fancy. Address the recipient with a formal Mr. or MS. Thank the interviewer for a great interview, and then describe what made it great. For example, you might mention the good exchange of ideas or

that you see the job as a wonderful opportunity. Add in a few of your ideas or mention something that you said in the interview that the interviewer liked. Complete your letter with the appropriate type of closing. "Sincerely", "Yours truly", or "gratefully" are acceptable for business letters.

In many ways, thank you letters may seem old fashion to you. You may be thinking a short email or a phone call will work just as well as a letter. This can be true when you need to correspond to someone that you know very well, but don't underestimate the power of a well-written thank you note. Letters go a long way to show your manners, sincerity, and attitude. They are easy to write and a great way to make a good impression.

53 **What is the main idea of the selection?**

A Hand written notes are better than emails.

B Always write a thank you note after a job interview.

C Thank you notes are a good way to show sincere appreciation.

D Thank you notes are hard to write but they show good manners.

54 **How is a business note different from a personal note?**

A A business note is more formal.

B A personal note is shorter.

C A business note should be hand written.

D A personal note should always be an email.

55 **Why is it to your advantage for the interviewer to remember your name?**

A They only hire people they know.

B They don't keep records of interviews.

C It will insure that you get the job.

D It may increase your chances for getting the job.

© Pearson Education, Inc., publishing as Pearson Prentice Hall. All rights reserved.

Name ______________________ Date ______________

ITBS PRACTICE TEST

Vocabulary

DIRECTIONS

This is a test about words and their meanings.

- For each question, you are to decide which one of the four answers has most nearly the same meaning as the underlined word above it.
- Then, on your answer folder, find the row of answer spaces numbered the same as the question. Fill in the answer space that has the same letter as the answer you picked.

The sample on this page shows you what the questions are like and how to mark your answers.

SAMPLE

S1 **Getting enough <u>exercise</u>**

A excitement
B work finished
C enjoyment of life
D movement of the body

ANSWER

S1 A B C **D**

© Pearson Education, Inc., publishing as Pearson Prentice Hall. All rights reserved.

Name ______________________ Date ______________

Vocabulary

1 **To <u>cease</u> fighting**

- **A** enjoy
- **B** avoid
- **C** receive
- **D** halt

2 **To tell an <u>anecdote</u>**

- **J** funny story
- **K** strong argument
- **L** riddle
- **M** untruth

3 **Discovered a <u>rarity</u>**

- **A** something underground
- **B** anything difficult
- **C** something uncommon
- **D** anything remembered

4 **A <u>genteel</u> officer**

- **J** polite
- **K** well-trained
- **L** well-armed
- **M** gruff

5 **The <u>nimble</u> mouse**

- **A** hungry
- **B** quick
- **C** tame
- **D** naughty

6 **He showed great <u>valor</u>.**

- **J** dancing skill
- **K** courage
- **L** sense of adventure
- **M** understanding

7 **A <u>petite</u> girl**

- **A** having good manners
- **B** dressing with style
- **C** short and thin
- **D** long and lean

8 **An <u>oath</u> given**

- **J** promise
- **K** gift
- **L** support
- **M** alarm

9 **<u>Genuine</u> leather**

- **A** tough
- **B** real
- **C** new
- **D** sold

10 **The police <u>relented</u>.**

- **J** patrolled
- **K** softened
- **L** continued
- **M** chased

11 **To <u>wreak</u> destruction**

- **A** break
- **B** escape
- **C** add to
- **D** carry out

12 **The glasses <u>cascaded</u>.**

- **J** broke into pieces
- **K** slid across
- **L** were cleaned
- **M** fell like water

13 **Full of <u>mirth</u>**

- **A** mixture
- **B** danger
- **C** happiness
- **D** togetherness

14 **An <u>outstanding</u> job**

- **J** difficult
- **K** long waited for
- **L** high quality
- **M** serious

© Pearson Education, Inc., publishing as Pearson Prentice Hall. All rights reserved.

Name ______________________ Date ______________

Reading Comprehension

DIRECTIONS

This is a test of how well you understand what you read.

- This test consists of reading passages followed by questions.
- Read each passage and then answer the questions.
- Four answers are given for each question. You are to choose the answer that you think is better than the others.
- Then, on your answer folder, find the row of answer spaces numbered the same as the question. Fill in the answer space for the best answer.

The sample on this page shows you what the questions are like and how to mark your answers.

SAMPLE

> Demi watched her new flying disk sink beneath the surface of the lake. She was not in a hurry to get home because she knew she would have to tell her father what happened. He had spent quite a bit of money on that doll.

S1 Why is Demi not in a hurry to get home?

A She wants to go and buy another doll.
B She is afraid her father will be angry.
C She is having a lot of fun at the lake.
D She wants to look for her doll in the lake.

ANSWER

S1 A **B** C D

© Pearson Education, Inc., publishing as Pearson Prentice Hall. All rights reserved.

Name ______________________ Date ______________

This is an excerpt from an adaptation of a speech by American Indian speaker and diplomat, Chief Seattle. Originally delivered in the 1850s, Chief Seattle's message was modified by screenwriter Ted Perry for use in a 1972 film about ecology.

¶1 The President in Washington sends word that he wishes to buy our land. But how can you buy or sell the sky? The land? The idea is strange to us. If we do not own the freshness of the air and the sparkle of the water, how can you buy them?

¶2 Every part of the earth is sacred to my people. Every shining pine needle, every sandy shore, every mist in the dark woods, every meadow, every humming insect. All are holy in the memory and experience of my people. . . .

¶3 The shining water that moves in the streams and rivers is not just water, but the blood of our ancestors. If we sell you our land, you must remember that it is sacred. Each ghostly reflection in the clear water of the lake tells of events and memories in the life of my people. The water's murmur is the voice of my father's father.

¶4 The rivers are our brothers. They quench our thirst. They carry our canoes and feed our children. So you must give the rivers the kindness you would give any brother.

¶5 If we sell you our land, remember that the air is precious to us, that the air shares its spirit with all the life it supports. The wind that gave our grandfather his first breath also receives his last sigh. The wind also gives our children the spirit of life. So if we sell you our land, you must keep it apart and sacred, as a place where man can go to taste the wind that is sweetened by the meadow flowers. . . .

¶6 This we know: The earth does not belong to man, man belongs to the earth. All things are connected like the blood which unites us all. Man did not weave the web of life, he is merely a strand in it. Whatever he does to the web, he does to himself. . . .

¶7 Your destiny is a mystery to us. What will happen when the buffalo are all slaughtered? The wild horses tamed? What will happen when the secret corners of the forest are heavy with the scent of many men and the view of the ripe hills is blotted by talking wires? Where will the thicket be? Gone! Where will the eagle be? Gone! And what is it to say goodbye to the swift pony and the hunt? The end of living and the beginning of survival.

¶8 When the last Red Man has vanished with his wilderness and his memory is only the shadow of a cloud moving across the prairie, will these shores and forests still be here? Will there be any of the spirit of my people left?

© Pearson Education, Inc., publishing as Pearson Prentice Hall. All rights reserved.

Name ____________________ Date ____________

1 What is the main idea of this essay?

A The memories of people are connected to their homeland.
B People should never try to sell land that belongs to their family.
C The spirits of Native Americans live on in the water and air.
D People should respect the land because it gives them life.

2 What is the effect of the writer asking questions in paragraphs 1, 7, and 8?

J It forces the reader to think more carefully about the ideas in the passage.
K It makes the reader wonder how much the writer knows about his subject.
L It challenges the reader to look for the answers somewhere in the paragraph.
M It persuades the reader to agree with the ideas in the passage.

3 What prompts the narrator to discuss how important the earth is to his people?

A Determination not to sell his land
B Appreciation for the beauty of the dark woods
C Concern for what whites will do to it
D Hope that his father's spirit will remain

4 Why does the narrator think the idea of buying land is so strange?

J The narrator has inherited land, not bought it.
K It is too hard to set a price on water and air.
L The narrator does not understand money.
M You cannot buy what is not owned.

5 How does the author of this essay feel about the earth?

A He is puzzled by its mysteries.
B He believes that it is sacred.
C He is worried that it will vanish.
D He wishes that he owned it.

6 What does the narrator think the white people will do after they have bought the land?

J Sell it
K Ruin it
L Work it
M Worship it

7 How does the author feel about white people?

A He does not know any of them.
B He does not believe them.
C He does not understand them.
D He does not like them.

8 In paragraph 7, what does "talking wires" mean?

J Television cables
K Clothes lines
L Telephone wires
M Radio wires

9 The tone of this essay is one of

A anger.
B melancholy.
C humor.
D mystery.

© Pearson Education, Inc., publishing as Pearson Prentice Hall. All rights reserved.

Reading Comprehension

Identity

Let them be as flowers,
always watered, fed, guarded, and
admired,
but harnessed to a pot of dirt.

I'd rather be a tall, ugly weed,
clinging on cliffs, like an eagle
wind-wavering above high, jagged rocks.

To have broken through the surface
of stone,
to live, to feel exposed to the madness
of the vast, eternal sky.
To be swayed by the breezes of an
ancient sea,
carrying my soul, my seed, beyond
the mountains of time
or into the abyss of the bizarre.

I'd rather be unseen, and if
then shunned by everyone,
than to be a pleasant-smelling flower,
growing in clusters in the fertile valley,
where they're praised, handled, and
plucked
by greedy, human hands.

I'd rather smell of musty, green stench
than of sweet, fragrant lilac.
If I could stand alone, strong and free,
I'd rather be a tall, ugly weed.

— *Julio Noboa Polanco*

10 **What point is the author of this poem attempting to make?**

- **J** To be beautiful is to be admired.
- **K** Beauty and comfort are nothing without freedom.
- **L** Breaking free from the everyday can make one crazy.
- **M** To stand up for something sets a person free.

11 **With which statement about the importance of friends would the author most likely agree?**

- **A** Real friends allow a person to be an individual.
- **B** Good friends will join a person who stands alone.
- **C** The best friends like the same things their friends do.
- **D** True friends admire a friend who acts as they do.

12 **The tone of this poem is one of**

- **J** bitterness.
- **K** revolution.
- **L** hope.
- **M** defiance.

13 **What does breaking through stone prove about the author?**

- **A** That he is destructive
- **B** That he is stubborn
- **C** That he is admired
- **D** That he is strong

14 **If the weed hanging on the cliff were a person, it would be**

- **J** noble.
- **K** intelligent.
- **L** independent.
- **M** friendly.

© Pearson Education, Inc., publishing as Pearson Prentice Hall. All rights reserved.

Name ______________________________ Date ______________

Reading Comprehension

This passage is from a 1973 speech by Alice Walker in which she remembers what seeing Dr. Martin Luther King, Jr., for the first time meant to her.

¶1 In 1960, my mother bought a television set . . . And then, one day, there appeared the face of Dr. Martin Luther King, Jr. What a funny name, I thought. At the moment I first saw him, he was being handcuffed and shoved into a police truck. He had dared to claim his rights as a native son, and had been arrested. He displayed no fear, but seemed calm and serene, unaware of his own extraordinary courage. His whole body, like his conscience, was at peace. . . .

¶2 He was The One, The Hero, The One Fearless Person for whom we had waited. I hadn't even realized before that we *had* been waiting for Martin Luther King, Jr., but we had. And I knew it for sure when my mother added his name to the list of people she prayed for every night.

¶3 I sometimes think that it was literally the prayers of people like my mother and father, who had bowed down in the struggle for such a long time, that kept Dr. King alive until five years ago. For years we went to bed praying for his life, and awoke with the question "Is the 'Lord' still here?"

¶4 The public acts of Dr. King you know. They are visible all around you. His voice you would recognize sooner than any other voice you have heard in this century—this in spite of the fact that certain municipal libraries, like the one in downtown Jackson, do not carry recordings of his speeches, and the librarians chuckle cruelly when asked why they do not.

¶5 You know, if you have read his books, that his is a complex and revolutionary philosophy that few people are capable of understanding fully or have the patience to embody in themselves. Which is our weakness, which is our loss. . . .

¶6 You know of the prizes and awards that he tended to think very little of. And you know of his concern for the disinherited: the American Indian, the Mexican-American, and the poor American white—for whom he cared very much. . . .

¶7 But add to all of these things the one thing that seems to me second to none in importance: He gave us back our heritage. He gave us back our homeland; the bones and dust of our ancestors, who may now sleep within our caring *and* our hearing. . . . He gave us full-time use of our woods, and restored our memories to those of us who were forced to run away, as realities we might each day enjoy and leave for our children.

¶8 He gave us continuity of place, without which community is ephemeral. He gave us home.

© Pearson Education, Inc., publishing as Pearson Prentice Hall. All rights reserved.

Name ______________________ Date ______________

15 **In paragraph 5, what does the word "embody" mean?**

A Wait one's turn
B Provide an example
C Discuss intelligently
D Invest wisely

16 **To whom is the narrator referring when she says that "we had waited"?**

J Native Americans
K African Americans
L The Walker Family
M The King Family

17 **From the author's description of the librarians in downtown Jackson, they are most likely**

A black.
B misunderstood.
C rich.
D white.

18 **When did the narrator realize that Dr. Martin Luther King, Jr., was such an important person?**

J When he began to receive his awards
K When her mother started praying for him
L When she first saw him on television
M When his first book was published

19 **In paragraph 6, what does the word "disinherited" mean?**

A Loss of property
B Not having a family
C Those without money
D Those deprived of rights

20 **Why would King's conscience have been "at peace"?**

J His conscience was part of his body, which was at peace.
K He felt hope that he would achieve what he fought for.
L He believed what he was fighting for was just.
M He believed in equality through peaceful means.

21 **In paragraph 7, what does the narrator mean when she says that King "gave us back our heritage"?**

A He made African Americans proud of where they came from.
B He took in African Americans who were homeless.
C He brought African traditions to blacks in America.
D He reminded them that their ancestors had been slaves.

22 **What was it about seeing King on television that the narrator thought was funny?**

J His name
K His courage
L His face
M His son

© Pearson Education, Inc., publishing as Pearson Prentice Hall. All rights reserved.

Name ______________________ Date ______________

Reading Comprehension

This piece comes from the story *The Dinner Party* by Mona Gardner.

¶1 . . . A large dinner party is being given in an up-country station by a colonial official and his wife. . . .

¶2 At one side of the long table a spirited discussion springs up between a young girl and a colonel. The girl insists women have long outgrown the jumping-on-a-chair-at-sight-of-a-mouse era, that they are not as fluttery as their grandmothers. The colonel says they are, explaining that women haven't the actual nerve control of men. . . .

¶3 "A woman's unfailing reaction in any crisis," the colonel says, "is to scream. And while a man may feel like it, yet he has that ounce more of control than a woman has. And that last ounce is what counts!"

¶4 The American scientist does not join in the argument, but sits watching the faces of the other guests. As he looks, he sees a strange expression come over the face of the hostess. She is staring straight ahead, the muscles of her face contracting slightly. With a small gesture she summons the native boy standing behind her chair. She whispers to him. The boy's eyes widen: he turns quickly and leaves the room. No one else sees this, nor the boy when he puts a bowl of milk on the verandah . . .

¶5 The American comes to with a start. In India, milk in a bowl means only one thing. It is bait for a snake. . . .

¶6 He looks up at the rafters . . . and sees they are bare. Three corners of the room, which he can see by shifting only slightly, are empty. In the fourth corner a group of servants stand . . . The American realizes there is only one place left—under the table.

¶7 His first impulse is to jump back and warn the others. But he knows the commotion will frighten the cobra and it will strike. He speaks quickly, the quality of his voice so arresting that it sobers everyone.

¶8 "I want to know just what control everyone at this table has. I will count three hundred . . . and not one of you is to move a single muscle. . . ."

¶9 The 20 people sit like stone images while he counts. . . . [H]e sees the cobra emerge and make for the bowl of milk. Four or five screams ring out as he jumps to slam shut the verandah doors.

¶10 "You certainly were right, Colonel!" the host says. "A man has just shown us an example of real control."

¶11 "Just a minute," the American says, turning to his hostess, "there's one thing I'd like to know. Mrs. Whynnes, how did you know that cobra was in the room?"

¶12 A faint smile lights up the woman's face as she replies. "Because it was lying across my foot."

© Pearson Education, Inc., publishing as Pearson Prentice Hall. All rights reserved.

Name ______________________________ Date ______________

23 The American scientist appears to be the type of person who likes to

A relax.
B investigate.
C take orders.
D take risks.

24 In paragraph 7, what does the phrase "so arresting that it sobers everyone" mean?

J So serious-sounding that it makes everyone laugh
K So beautiful-sounding that it makes everyone melancholy
L So legal-sounding that everyone gets frightened
M So important-sounding that everyone pays attention

25 What is the effect of putting the argument about self-control at the beginning of the story?

A It provides ideas for the reader to consider while reading the rest of the story.
B It causes surprise when it is revealed that a woman had such self-control.
C It creates more sympathy for the American, who is not allowed to participate.
D It distracts everyone in the story so that the cobra may sneak into the room.

26 Why does the hostess call to the boy waiting behind her chair?

J There is a cobra on her foot.
K The next course of the meal is ready.
L She wants another bowl of milk for her guests.
M She wants him to check on the American.

27 How does the American know the milk is for a cobra when he has not yet seen the snake?

A There are no other pets in the house.
B He could smell the poison cobras have.
C Milk is used as cobra bait in India.
D He asks the serving boy.

28 What is the author's view of the American scientist?

J He has more respect for women than most men.
K He has more self-control than most men.
L His great heroism saves everyone at the party.
M His training as a scientist makes him a valuable guest.

29 Which character in the story is named Whynnes?

A The American
B The hostess
C The serving boy
D The young girl

30 In paragraph 9, what does "sit like stone images" mean?

J Pose for pictures
K Remain very still
L Sit very straight
M Wait for dessert

© Pearson Education, Inc., publishing as Pearson Prentice Hall. All rights reserved.

Name ______________________ Date ______________

Spelling

DIRECTIONS

This test will show how well you can spell.

- Many of the questions in this test contain mistakes in spelling. Some do not have any mistakes at all.
- You should look for mistakes in spelling.
- When you find a mistake, fill in the answer space on your answer folder that has the same letter as the **line** containing the mistake.
- If there is no mistake, fill in the last answer space.

The samples on this page show you what the questions are like and how to mark your answers.

SAMPLES

S1
- **A** crisp
- **B** bright
- **C** washed
- **D** appel
- **E** (No mistakes)

S2
- **J** silver
- **K** copper
- **L** bronze
- **M** nickel
- **N** *(No mistakes)*

ANSWERS

S1 A B C **D** E

S2 J K L M **N**

© Pearson Education, Inc., publishing as Pearson Prentice Hall. All rights reserved.

Name ______________________ Date ______________

Spelling

1
A ligten
B glitch
C thorough
D borrow
E *(No mistakes)*

2
J stallion
K oriental
L accidentel
M tournament
N *(No mistakes)*

3
A trophy
B ability
C catastrophe
D commitee
E *(No mistakes)*

4
J reproduce
K proportion
L installation
M lettuce
N *(No mistakes)*

5
A indignant
B severance
C preparation
D allowense
E *(No mistakes)*

6
J tremendous
K torrential
L pourous
M emperor
N *(No mistakes)*

7
A tremble
B tenous
C extend
D delirious
E *(No mistakes)*

8
J incidental
K practicing
L galactic
M significant
N *(No mistakes)*

9
A gaget
B rocket
C hatchet
D college
E *(No mistakes)*

10
J invisible
K fairy
L totalety
M entirety
N *(No mistakes)*

11
A nibbled
B antelope
C cantalope
D builder
E *(No mistakes)*

12
J energize
K anesthesia
L gypsy
M incapible
N *(No mistakes)*

13
A dabbling
B gossiped
C irresistible
D graple
E *(No mistakes)*

14
J hereditary
K ordinery
L intrigue
M boredom
N *(No mistakes)*

© Pearson Education, Inc., publishing as Pearson Prentice Hall. All rights reserved.

Name ______________________________ Date ______________

Capitalization

DIRECTIONS

This is a test on capitalization. It will show how well you can use capital letters in sentences.

- You should look for mistakes in capitalization in the sentences on this test.
- When you find a mistake, fill in the answer space on your answer folder that has the same letter as the **line** containing the mistake.
- Some sentences do not have any mistakes at all. If there is no mistake, fill in the last answer space.

The samples on this page show you what the questions are like and how to mark your answers.

SAMPLES

S1
A My birthday is on
B june 25, and I am
C having a party.
D *(No mistakes)*

S2
J My Aunt asked
K my cousin to bring
L his pet horse.
M *(No mistakes)*

S3
A The horse's name
B is Lightfoot, and he
C is an Arabian.
D *(No mistakes)*

ANSWERS

S1 A **B** C D
S2 **J** K L M
S3 A B C **D**

© Pearson Education, Inc., publishing as Pearson Prentice Hall. All rights reserved.

Name ______________________________ Date ______________

Capitalization

1 **A** Although Mark Twain traveled
B widely, his boyhood experiences
C on the Mississippi river affected him most.
D *(No mistakes)*

2 **J** The Congress avenue bridge
K is home to the largest urban colony of bats.
L I have tried but never suceeded in seeing them.
M *(No mistakes)*

3 **A** Every Saturday night, more than two million
B listeners tune in to Garrison Keillor's
C radio show, "A Prairie Home Companion."
D *(No mistakes)*

4 **J** For years, astronauts have conducted
K experiments to learn about living in
L space, maybe even on the Moon.
M *(No mistakes)*

5 **A** The underground Railroad was a network
B of people who helped slaves escape from
C the South in the mid-1800s.
D *(No mistakes)*

6 **J** Many of the Pilgrims who first came to
K America were members of the puritan
L sect, who were unpopular in England.
M *(No mistakes)*

7 **A** I find some of the strangest people
B enjoy listening to AM radio. stranger
C ones still listen to the FM stuff.
D *(No mistakes)*

8 **J** The Yukon Territory is in the
K northwestern corner of Canada,
L just beside alaska.
M *(No mistakes)*

9 **A** History's largest gold rush took place
B in august of 1896 near a river
C called Dawson's Creek.
D *(No mistakes)*

10 **J** Taiwan has been occupied by Portugal,
K China, Holland, and Japan. Today, it is
L home to many who fled Mainland China.
M *(No mistakes)*

11 **A** Langston Hughes published his first
B collection of poetry, *The Weary blues,*
C in 1926. By 1930, he was famous.
D *(No mistakes)*

12 **J** One of Russia's, and perhaps the world's,
K greatest writers, Leo Tolstoy, died
L seven years before the Russian revolution.
M *(No mistakes)*

© Pearson Education, Inc., publishing as Pearson Prentice Hall. All rights reserved.

Name ______________________ Date ______________

Punctuation

DIRECTIONS

This is a test on punctuation. It will show how well you can use periods, question marks, commas, and other kinds of punctuation marks.

- You should look for mistakes in punctuation in the sentences on this test.
- When you find a mistake, fill in the answer space on your answer folder that has the same letter as the **line** containing the mistake.
- Some sentences do not have any mistakes at all. If there is no mistake, fill in the last answer space.

The samples on this page show you what the questions are like and how to mark your answers.

SAMPLES

S1 **A** When he spotted the
B water fountain, Bill
C said, "Finally!"
D *(No mistakes)*

S2 **J** How long had he been
K running? He was too
L tired to remember?
M *(No mistakes)*

S3 **A** He knew he had started
B at 8:00 A.M, but what
C time was it now?
D *(No mistakes)*

ANSWERS

S1 A B C **D**
S2 J K **L** M
S3 A **B** C D

© Pearson Education, Inc., publishing as Pearson Prentice Hall. All rights reserved.

Name ______________________ Date ____________

Punctuation

1 **A** Carved into a peak, Mount Rushmore has the
B heads of four U.S. presidents Washington,
C Jefferson, Lincoln, and Teddy Roosevelt.
D *(No mistakes)*

2 **J** In 1936, the United States was in
K the middle of the Great Depression a time
L of economic struggle.
M *(No mistakes)*

3 **A** Between 1892 and 1924 more than
B 12,000,000 immigrants entered the
C United States through Ellis Island.
D *(No mistakes)*

4 **J** Carl Sandburg said of Americans
K during the Great Depression "The people
L will live on . . . and come back."
M *(No mistakes)*

5 **A** On a trip from California to New York,
B John Steinbeck passed through the Mojave
C Desert; Texas; and the Deep South.
D *(No mistakes)*

6 **J** Carhenge is a replica of Stonehenge.
K It is built entirely out of American
L cars stacked on top of each other
M *(No mistakes)*

7 **A** Dear Allan and Julia Stiles.
B I am very sorry for your loss,
C and I know things will be better soon.
D *(No mistakes)*

8 **J** "Tell them I hope the funeral is just
K beautiful, was what Mom said, and
L then she just started crying again.
M *(No mistakes)*

9 **A** Skippy was a good friend and a loyal
B companion. so full of life and love that
C it seemed he would live forever.
D *(No mistakes)*

10 **J** Can you ever love another dog
K I certainly hope so because
L I'm sending along a new friend for you.
M *(No mistakes)*

11 **A** The puppy's name is Winston, and he
B licks your face just the way Skippy did.
C He eats puppy food now, but he's growing.
D *(No mistakes)*

12 **J** Try to write back and tell me what you think.
K With much love
L Wendy Jackson
M *(No mistakes)*

© Pearson Education, Inc., publishing as Pearson Prentice Hall. All rights reserved.

Name ______________________________ Date ______________

Usage and Expression

PART 1 DIRECTIONS

This is a test on the use of words. It will show how well you can use words according to the standards of correctly written English.

- You should look for mistakes in the sentences on this test.
- When you find a mistake, fill in the answer space on your answer folder that has the same letter as the **line** containing the mistake.
- Some sentences do not have any mistakes at all. If there is no mistake, fill in the last answer space.

The samples on this page show you what the questions are like and how to mark your answers.

SAMPLES

S1
A If dogs are called man's
B best friend, shouldn't
C it be nice to men?
D *(No mistakes)*

S2
J I have had three dogs
K in my life, and not one
L of them has liked me.
M *(No mistakes)*

ANSWERS

S1 A B **C** D

S2 J K L **M**

© Pearson Education, Inc., publishing as Pearson Prentice Hall. All rights reserved.

Name ______________________ Date ______________

Usage

1 **A** A symbolic shadow fell across the country
B when war breaks out between the northern
C and southern states in 1861.
D *(No mistakes)*

2 **J** The couple stopped to look at
K the flock of gooses rising from the pond
L in one tremendous swoop.
M *(No mistakes)*

3 **A** Eated for hours made Edward so
B thirsty that he drank four sodas,
C three milkshakes, and a gallon of milk.
D *(No mistakes)*

4 **J** Mushrooms are a type of fungus. As long as
K much needed minerals, climate, and moisture
L are provided, mushrooms can live for years.
M *(No mistakes)*

5 **A** Whenever I make a mistake, I try to get
B the grip on where was it I went wrong.
C This helps me figure out how to fix it.
D *(No mistakes)*

6 **J** Alice was very tired after she bringed
K fifteen bags of groceries back from the
L store and put them all away.
M *(No mistakes)*

7 **A** The recipe called for two cups of Swiss
B cheese, so Maria searched in the top
C cupboard for her cheese grater.
D *(No mistakes)*

8 **J** "Try not to eat them tomatoes," Gary's
K father warned him. "They've been sitting
L in the chicken coop for hours."
M *(No mistakes)*

9 **A** A bat is a mammal, meaning that its
B young are born live, not hatched, and get
C its milk from its mothers.
D *(No mistakes)*

10 **J** Evan was being made tired and cranky
K by the constant spinning and whirling
L of the empty clothes dryer.
M *(No mistakes)*

11 **A** Creative more than a hundred years ago,
B Sherlock Holmes is as popular as ever,
C appearing in countless films and plays.
D *(No mistakes)*

12 **J** One of those brand new gelatin machines
K are being delivered to my parents' house,
L and they said I get to try it first.
M *(No mistakes)*

© Pearson Education, Inc., publishing as Pearson Prentice Hall. All rights reserved.

Name ______________________ Date ______________

Expression

PART 2 DIRECTIONS

This is Part 2 of the test about the use of words. It will show how well you can express ideas correctly and effectively. There are several sections to this part of the test. Read the directions to each section carefully. Then mark your answers on your answer folder.

Directions: In questions 13–19, choose the best way to express the idea.

13
- **A** The two boys hunted through the entire toy store without finding the dolls.
- **B** The two boys through the entire toy store hunted without finding the dolls.
- **C** The two boys hunted, without finding, through the entire toy store the dolls.
- **D** The two boys, without finding the dolls, hunted through the entire toy store.

14
- **J** Before going to bed, he finished his sandwich.
- **K** He finished his sandwich, and then he decided to go to bed.
- **L** Even though he was going to bed, he felt like he needed to finish his sandwich.
- **M** Before going to bed, his sandwich was finished.

15
- **A** Beth saw a woman looking at her mother, who was too good for this world.
- **B** Beth saw a woman looking at her mother who was too good for this world.
- **C** Looking at her mother, Beth saw a woman too good for this world.
- **D** Too good for this world, Beth's mother saw a woman looking.

16
- **J** Going on a hike and bike riding are Joan's favorite outdoor activities.
- **K** Hiking and bike riding are Joan's favorite outdoor activities.
- **L** Joan's favorite outdoor activities are hiking and a ride on her bike.
- **M** Joan's favorite outdoor activities are a hike and a bike.

© Pearson Education, Inc., publishing as Pearson Prentice Hall. All rights reserved.

Name ____________________ Date ____________________

17 A The door shut with a crash. The door squeaked loudly.

B The door shut with a crash, loudly squeaking.

C Crashing loudly, the door squeaked shut.

D The door squeaked loudly and then shut with a crash.

18 J Running in the park, Dave's son saw a squirrel, and he chased him.

K Dave's son saw a squirrel, and Dave chased him in the park.

L Running in the park, Dave's son chased him and a squirrel.

M Dave chased his son running after a squirrel in the park.

19 A Clowns that don't have big noses, usually has huge feet.

B Clowns without big noses usually have huge feet.

C Clowns that had huge feet usually end up not having big noses.

D Clowns without big noses were clowns without having huge feet.

20 **Which of these is the best advertisement for a big shoe sale?**

J All sneakers, pumps, and boots in the store are up to 75% off.

K Up to 75 shoes are on sale, from sneakers to boots to pumps.

L If you go one place to buy shoes, come to the place where they are cheap.

M A 75% off sale is going on this weekend only; everything must go.

© Pearson Education, Inc., publishing as Pearson Prentice Hall. All rights reserved.

Name ______________________ Date ______________

TERRANOVA PRACTICE TEST

Reading and Language Arts

Sample Passage

Volunteers

In communities across the nation, people volunteer and improve the lives of others. Some volunteering opportunities can be found through organizations—serving food in a soup kitchen, working with a group to teach adults to read, or joining others to build houses for those who might not otherwise be able to afford them. In contrast, some volunteering opportunities are not organized. People may take groceries to their elderly neighbors, or a few adults might get together to help a mother of triplets manage her newborns.

Sample A

This passage is mostly about

Ⓐ why people volunteer

Ⓑ how people can volunteer

Ⓒ how people benefit from volunteering

Ⓓ why volunteer programs save money

© Pearson Education, Inc., publishing as Pearson Prentice Hall. All rights reserved.

Name ______________________________ Date ______________

Directions

A student wrote a paragraph about volunteering at a local nursing home. There are some mistakes that need correcting.

> **1** Last summer I volunteered one day a week at the Sunshine Retirement Center. **2** Some days I helped change sheets and deliver meals, and other days I just spending time talking to the residents. **3** Even though the summer volunteer program is over and I'm back in school, I still stop by to spend time with the people there.

Sample B

Choose the best way to write Sentence 2.

- Ⓕ Some days I helped change sheets and deliver meals, and other days I just spent time talking to the residents.
- Ⓖ Some days I helped change sheets and delivered meals, and other days I just spending time talking to the residents.
- Ⓗ Some days I helping change sheets and delivering meals, and other days I just spending time talking to the residents.
- Ⓙ Best as it is

Sample C

Which sentence would best follow Sentence 2?

- Ⓐ It took a lot of my time.
- Ⓑ It was more rewarding than I could have ever imagined.
- Ⓒ I don't like doing that much work if I'm not being graded.
- Ⓓ I think that next year I'll do some other kind of volunteering.

© Pearson Education, Inc., publishing as Pearson Prentice Hall. All rights reserved.

Name ______________________________ Date ______________

The Wonders of Technology

When you talk on the telephone, watch television, send e-mail, or use a computer, you depend on technology to perform your task. *Technology* is the application of human skill. Technology can be as simple as a pen and paper or as complicated as the inner workings of a computer. Technology is continually changing. New and better ways of doing things are developed every day.

In this theme, you will read about some ways technology is used—and overused. Start reading and begin to learn more about **The Wonders of Technology.**

from E-Mail from Bill Gates *by* John Seabrook

Directions

In this excerpt, John Seabrook describes how he corresponded with Bill Gates via e-mail while gathering information for a magazine article. Ongoing correspondence between the two reveals Gates's philosophy about technology. Read the excerpt. Then do numbers 1 through 6.

At the moment, the best way to communicate with another person on the information highway[1] is to exchange electronic mail: to write a message on a computer and send it through the telephone lines into someone else's computer. In the future, people will send each other sound and pictures as well as text, and do it in real time,[2] and improved technology will make it possible to have rich, human electronic exchanges, but at present E-mail is the closest thing we have to that. Even now, E-mail allows you to meet and communicate with people in a way that would be impossible on the phone, through the regular mail, or face to face, as I discovered while I was working on this story. Sitting at my computer one day, I realized that I could try to communicate with Bill Gates, the chairman and co-founder of the software giant Microsoft, on the information highway. At least, I could send E-mail to his electronic address, which is widely available, not tell anyone at Microsoft I was doing it, and see what happened. I wrote:

Dear Bill,

I am the guy who is writing the article about you for The New Yorker. It occurs to me that we ought to be able to do some of the work through e-mail. Which raises the fascinating question—What kind of understanding of another person can e-mail give you? . . .

You could begin by telling me what you think is unique about e-mail as a form of communication.

John

I hit "return," and the computer said, "mail sent." I walked out to the kitchen to get a drink of water and played with the cat for a while, then came back and sat at my computer. Thinking that I was probably wasting money, I nevertheless logged on again and entered my password. "You have mail," the computer said.

I typed "get mail," and the computer got the following:

From: Bill Gates
<billg@microsoft.com>
Ok, let me know if you get this email.

According to my computer, eighteen minutes had passed between the time I E-mailed Bill and he E-mailed me back. His message said:

© Pearson Education, Inc., publishing as Pearson Prentice Hall. All rights reserved.

Name ______________________________ Date ______________

E-mail is a unique communication vehicle for a lot of reasons. However, email is not a substitute for direct interaction. . . .

There are people who I have corresponded with on email for months before actually meeting them—people at work and otherwise. If someone isn't saying something of interest its easier to not respond to their mail than it is not to answer the phone. In fact I give out my home phone number to almost no one but my email address is known very broadly. I am the only person who reads my email so no one has to worry about embarrassing themselves or going around people when they send a message. Our email is completely secure. . . .

Email helps out with other types of communication. It allows you to exchange a lot of information in advance of a meeting and make the meeting far more valuable. . . .

Email is not a good way to get mad at someone since you can't interact. You can send friendly messages very easily since those are harder to misinterpret.

We began to E-mail each other three or four times a week. I would have a question about something and say to myself, "I'm going to E-mail Bill about that," and I'd write him a message and get a one- or two-page message back within twenty-four hours, sometimes much sooner. At the beginning of our electronic relationship, I would wake up in the middle of the night and lie in bed wondering if I had E-mail from Bill. Generally, he seemed to write messages at night, sleep (maybe), then send them the next morning. We were intimate in a curious way, in the sense of being wired into each other's minds, but our contact was elaborately stylized, like ballroom dancing.

[1]**Information highway:** Network of computers and file servers that allows for the rapid exchange of electronic information.

[2]**real time:** Accessing of information or exchange of data that requires no downloading of files.

Here is a time line of what happens in the passage.

Author asks Bill Gates a question by e-mail.	Author checks his e-mail.	?	Author and Bill Gates e-mail each other regularly.

1 **Which of these should go in the empty box in the time line?**

Ⓐ Author wakes up in the middle of the night.

Ⓑ Author decides not to tell Microsoft that he e-mails Bill Gates.

Ⓒ Author reads answer from Bill Gates.

Ⓓ Author decides to write article for *The New Yorker.*

© Pearson Education, Inc., publishing as Pearson Prentice Hall. All rights reserved.

Name ______________________________ Date ______________________

2 Choose the sentence that best describes what the passage is mainly about.

Ⓕ E-mail is a great way to gather research for an article.

Ⓖ E-mail allows you to communicate with people in a special way.

Ⓗ While e-mail is a great way to communicate, it has its limitations.

Ⓙ Even very busy people like Bill Gates enjoy sending and receiving e-mail.

3 From evidence in the passage, which of these descriptions best fits Bill Gates?

Ⓐ He tries to help the author.

Ⓑ He is nervous about being interviewed.

Ⓒ He wishes the author would call him on the phone.

Ⓓ He expects the author to be intimidated by his success.

4 According to the passage, e-mail is helpful for business meetings because it

Ⓕ eliminates the need to meet in person

Ⓖ helps you take notes during the meeting

Ⓗ helps you process requests more quickly

Ⓙ allows you to exchange information beforehand

5 According to the passage, Bill Gates responds to the author's e-mail

Ⓐ sometimes

Ⓑ very quickly

Ⓒ after a long wait

Ⓓ before the author is ready

6 In the passage, Bill Gates says, "email is not a substitute for direct interaction." The word *interaction* means

Ⓕ contact

Ⓖ leisure time

Ⓗ private thought

Ⓙ telephone conversation

© Pearson Education, Inc., publishing as Pearson Prentice Hall. All rights reserved.

Name ______________________________ Date ______________________

The Internet

Directions

Mrs. Anderson's class is writing about different kinds of technology. Josh wrote about the Internet, a worldwide computer network. There are several mistakes that need correcting. Here is the first part of his report.

> [1]What is the Internet? [2]I have to admit that before I started writing this report. [3]I really wasn't sure. [4]The Internet is the largest computer network on the planet. [5]A network is a group of computers linked together to share information. [6]The network of computers grouped together to make up the Internet connects over 20 million computers!

7 Sentence 2 is not a complete sentence. Which of these best combines it with Sentence 3?

- Ⓐ Before I started writing this report, I really wasn't sure I have to admit.
- Ⓑ Before I started writing this report, I have to admit that I really wasn't sure of that.
- Ⓒ I have to admit that before I started writing this report, I really wasn't sure.
- Ⓓ I have to admit that I really wasn't sure and that's why I started writing this report.

8 Which is the best way to write Sentence 6?

- Ⓕ The computer network that makes up the Internet connects over 20 million computers!
- Ⓖ The Internet connects over 20 million computers with the computers that make up its network.
- Ⓗ The network of computers that are grouped together to form the Internet connects over 20 million computers!
- Ⓙ Best as it is

© Pearson Education, Inc., publishing as Pearson Prentice Hall. All rights reserved.

Name ______________________________ Date ______________

Now read the second part of the report.

[1]The United States Department of Defense started the Internet in the 1960s so that researchers in different parts of the country could communicate and exchange information. [2]In addition to work, these researchers discussed all kinds of things on the Internet. [3]It wasn't long before their friends started using the Internet. [4]Some of their families used it too. [5]By the 1990s, the Internet was huge and real popular. [6]Today, anyone with a computer and a modem can access the Internet.

9 Where would this sentence best fit in the paragraph?

They talked about the Rolling Stones, flying kites, friends, and other things that interested them.

- (A) after Sentence 1
- (B) after Sentence 2
- (C) after Sentence 3
- (D) after Sentence 5

10 Which is the best way to write Sentence 5?

- (F) Huge and popular the Internet was by the 1990s.
- (G) By the 1990s, the huge Internet was real popular.
- (H) By the 1990s, the Internet was huge and really popular.
- (J) Best as it is

© Pearson Education, Inc., publishing as Pearson Prentice Hall. All rights reserved.

Name ______________________ Date ______________________

Here is the last part of the report.

[1]Today, you can use the Internet for all kinds of things. [2]I used it to research this report. [3]I also used it to help me with a science project. [4]The Internet is like having a gigantic library at your fingertips—all you have to do to enter it is click your mouse! [5]Researchers believe that in the future every single house on the planet has a computer and will have access to the Internet.

11 Which is the best way to combine Sentences 2 and 3 into one?

- (A) I used the Internet to research this report and help me with a science project.
- (B) I used the Internet to research this report, I also used it to help me with a science project.
- (C) I used the Internet to research this report, but I also used it to help me with a science project.
- (D) While I used the Internet to research this report, I also used it to help me with a science project.

12 The best way to write Sentence 5 is

- (F) Researchers believe that in the future every house on the planet will have a computer and access to the Internet.
- (G) Researchers believe that in the future every house on the planet, having a computer and access to the Internet.
- (H) Researchers believe that, on the planet, most houses in the future will have a computer and will have access to the Internet.
- (J) Best as it is

© Pearson Education, Inc., publishing as Pearson Prentice Hall. All rights reserved.

Name ______________________________ Date ______________

from The Trouble with Television *by* Robert MacNeil

Directions

Here is an excerpt from an essay by Robert MacNeil, a former broadcast journalist. In the essay, MacNeil explains why he believes TV threatens the development of our language, literacy, and imagination.

The trouble with television is that it discourages concentration. Almost anything interesting and rewarding in life requires some constructive, consistently applied effort. The dullest, the least gifted of us can achieve things that seem miraculous to those who never concentrate on anything. But television encourages us to apply no effort. It sells us instant gratification. It diverts us only to divert, to make the time pass without pain.

Television's variety becomes a narcotic,[1] not a stimulus.[2] Its serial, kaleidoscopic[3] exposures force us to follow its lead. The viewer is on a perpetual guided tour: thirty minutes at the museum, thirty at the cathedral, then back on the bus to the next attraction—except on television, typically, the spans allotted are on the order of minutes or seconds, and the chosen delights are more often car crashes and people killing one another. In short, a lot of television usurps one of the most precious of all human gifts, the ability to focus your attention yourself, rather than just passively surrendering it.

Capturing your attention—and holding it—is the prime motive of most television programming and enhances its role as a profitable advertising vehicle. Programmers live in constant fear of losing anyone's attention—anyone's. The surest way to avoid doing so is to keep everything brief, not to strain the attention of anyone but instead to provide constant stimulation through variety, novelty, action and movement. Quite simply, television operates on the appeal to the short attention span. . . .

. . . In its place that is fine. Who can quarrel with a medium that so brilliantly packages escapist entertainment as a mass-marketing tool? But I see its values now pervading this nation and its life. It has become fashionable to think that, like fast food, fast ideas are the way to get to a fast-moving, impatient public.

In the case of news, this practice, in my view, results in inefficient communication. I question how much of television's nightly news effort is really absorbable and understandable. Much of it is what has been aptly described as "machine gunning with scraps." I think its technique fights coherence.[4] I think it tends to make things ultimately boring and dismissable (unless they are accompanied by horrifying pictures) because almost anything is boring and dismissable if you know almost nothing about it.

I believe that TV's appeal to the short attention span is not only inefficient communication but decivilizing as well. Consider the casual assumptions that television tends to cultivate: that complexity must be avoided, that visual stimulation is a substitute for thought, that verbal precision is an anachronism.[5] It may be old-fashioned, but I was taught that thought is words, arranged in grammatically precise ways.

[1]**narcotic** (när kät´ ik) *n.:* Something that has a soothing effect.

[2]**stimulus** (stim´ yə ləs) *n.:* Something that rouses to action.

[3]**kaleidoscopic** (kə li´ də skäp´ ik) *adj.:* Constantly changing.

[4]**coherence** (kō hir´ əns) *n.:* The quality of being connected in an intelligible way.

[5]**anachronism** (ə nak´ rə niz´ əm) *n.:* Anything that seems to be out of its proper place in history.

© Pearson Education, Inc., publishing as Pearson Prentice Hall. All rights reserved.

Name ______________________ Date ______________

13 What is the major purpose of this essay?

Ⓐ to reveal little-known facts about television

Ⓑ to persuade readers that television is harmful

Ⓒ to teach readers how to live without television

Ⓓ to entertain readers with stories about television

14 In the passage, the author says that television "sells us instant gratification." The word *gratification* probably means

Ⓕ information

Ⓖ interpretation

Ⓗ observation

Ⓙ satisfaction

15 The author believes television news may be difficult to understand because

Ⓐ too much violence is shown

Ⓑ too much advertising is on the news

Ⓒ the news is shown too quickly

Ⓓ the anchors use complicated language

16 In the passage, the author says that television "diverts us only to divert, to make the time pass without pain." The word *divert* means

Ⓕ inform

Ⓖ dismiss

Ⓗ distract

Ⓙ instruct

17 The author of this passage would probably agree that

Ⓐ people are generally very patient

Ⓑ television enhances concentration

Ⓒ television helps us focus on ourselves

Ⓓ people should spend more time reading

© Pearson Education, Inc., publishing as Pearson Prentice Hall. All rights reserved.

Name ______________________________ Date ______________

from How to be Polite Online *by* Virginia Shea

Directions

Here is an excerpt from "How to be Polite Online," an essay by Virginia Shea. In the excerpt, Shea offers tips and guidelines to help computer users communicate more effectively and courteously online.

The truth is that computer networking is still in its infancy. Probably nothing illustrates this more clearly than the "ASCII[1] jail": 90 percent of network communications are still limited to plain old ASCII text—that is, the characters of the alphabet, the numerals 0 through 9, and the most basic punctuation marks. It's bad enough that multimedia communications have not been implemented in most of cyberspace.[2] Most of the time you can't even put a word in bold or italics!

Because people cannot see or hear you in cyberspace, you need to pay close attention to the style of your electronic communications if you hope to make a good impression there. The style of electronic communications encompasses everything about your correspondence except its content, from your use of network conventions like "smileys" and "sigs" to the number of characters per line in your email messages.

Style considerations are influenced by several of the rules of Netiquette, especially Rule 4, Respect other people's time, and Rule 5, Make yourself look good online. It doesn't matter how brilliant your messages are if they're formatted in such a way that no one can read them.

Tone of voice online

The fact that most network interactions are limited to written words can be the source of misunderstandings. Fortunately, clever network users have had years to deal with this. They've created a shorthand to help communicate the tone that you'd otherwise get from the other person's voice, facial expressions, and gestures. These shorthand expressions are known as smileys or emoticons. They're easy to figure out once you get the hang of it. Just remember that they're all sideways faces.

See Table 1 for a list of the most commonly used emoticons. There are whole books about smileys for those who are interested, including the enjoyable *Smiley Dictionary* by Seth Godin.

People also use abbreviations to express emotional states or to qualify what they're saying. See Table 2 for a list of common abbreviations.

The "FLAME ON/FLAME OFF" notifier

When you really want to run off at the keyboard—but you want your readers to know that that you're not expressing yourself in your usual measured, reasoned manner—you need to let them know that you know that you're flaming.[3] So before you begin your rant, simply enter the words FLAME ON. Then rant away. When you're done, write FLAME OFF and resume normal discourse.

[1]**ASCII:** Abbreviation of American Standard Code for Information Interchange, a standard computer code used to assist the interchange of information among various types of data-processing equipment.

[2]**cyberspace:** Global communication performed through the use of computer technology.

[3]**flaming:** Slang for "ranting."

© Pearson Education, Inc., publishing as Pearson Prentice Hall. All rights reserved.

Name ______________________ Date ______________

Table 1: Emoticons	
:-)	Smile; laugh; "I'm joking"
:-(	Frown; sadness; "Bummer"
:)	Variant of :-) or "Have a nice day"
:(	Variant of :-(
;-)	Wink; denotes a pun or sly joke
:-O	Yelling or screaming; or completely shocked
:-()	Can't (or won't) stop talking
:-D	Big, delighted grin
:-P	Sticking out your tongue
:-] or :-)	Sarcastic smile
%-)	Confused but happy
%-(	Confused and unhappy
:'-(	Crying
:'-)	Crying happy tears
:-I	Can't decide how to feel; no feelings either way
:-\	Mixed but mostly happy
:-/	Mixed but mostly sad
*	Kiss
{} or [ ]	Hug
{{{***}}}	Hugs and kisses

Table 2: Abbreviations	
BTW	By the way
IMHO	In my humble opinion
IMNSHO	In my not so humble opinion
IOW	In other words
IRL	In real life
ITRW	In the real world
LOL	Laughing out loud
OTF	On the floor (laughing)
ROTFL	Rolling on the floor laughing
WRT	With regard to
YMMV	Your mileage may vary
<g> or <G>	Grin
<bg>	Big grin

© Pearson Education, Inc., publishing as Pearson Prentice Hall. All rights reserved.

Name ______________________________ Date ______________

18 **Look over the passage again. Choose the sentence that gives a clue that email sometimes causes confusion. Write the sentence on the lines below.**

____

____

Now write the sentence in your own words.

____

____

Write a message to a friend on the lines below. Use at least two emoticons and two abbreviations.

____

____

____

____

19 **A student used the Internet to research and write this paragraph about volcanoes. She made five mistakes in grammar, capitalization, and punctuation. Draw a line through each part that has a mistake, and write the correction above it.**

A volcano is a vent in the surface of the earth through which hot gases and ashes sometimes flows. When the gases and ashes flow out of the top of a volcano. It's said to be active. When this activity stops, the Volcano is considered dormant. One of the most famousest volcanoes is Mt. St. Helen's in Washington. After being dormant for over 120 years, the volcano erupted on May 18, 1980. While the major activity has stop, Mt. St. Helen's is still considered active.

© Pearson Education, Inc., publishing as Pearson Prentice Hall. All rights reserved.

Name ______________________________ Date ______________

20 Look back at the essay "The Trouble with Television" and think about how watching too much TV can be harmful. Now think about "E-Mail from Bill Gates." When can sending and receiving e-mail be harmful? Write a paragraph explaining your answer. Be sure to support your opinion with examples from either "The Trouble with Television" or "E-Mail from Bill Gates."

For this answer, make sure you use complete sentences and check your work for correct spelling, capitalization, and punctuation.

© Pearson Education, Inc., publishing as Pearson Prentice Hall. All rights reserved.

Name ______________________________ Date ______________

SAT 10 PRACTICE TEST

Vocabulary

Directions:

Look at each underlined word. Choose the word or group of words that means about the same thing.

1 A <u>volume</u> is a—

A bottle

B book

C storm

D map

2 To <u>remain</u> is to—

F stay

G keep

H travel

J buy

3 <u>Circumference</u> refers to—

A how tall

B how long

C how far around

D how heavy

4 <u>Speedily</u> means—

F quickly

G recently

H accurately

J carefully

Directions:

Read each boxed sentence. Then read the sentences that follow. Choose the sentence that uses the underlined word in the same way as in the box.

5

Steel contains <u>iron</u> and carbon.

In which sentence does the word <u>iron</u> mean the same thing as in the sentence above?

A Use an <u>iron</u> to press your skirt.

B <u>Iron</u> is a metallic element.

C Greg was stubborn and had an <u>iron</u> will.

D The ranchers marked the cattle with a branding <u>iron</u>.

6

The playground is in a bad <u>state</u> of repair.

In which sentence does the word <u>state</u> mean the same thing as in the sentence above?

F Alabama was the 22nd <u>state</u> to join the union.

G Please <u>state</u> your name and age.

H Keiko was in a <u>state</u> of excitement on her birthday.

J You should <u>state</u> your intentions.

© Pearson Education, Inc., publishing as Pearson Prentice Hall. All rights reserved.

Name ______________________ Date ______________________

Reading Comprehension

from "Shooting Stars" by Hal Borland

Directions:

Read this excerpt from "Shooting Stars" by Hal Borland. Then complete numbers 1 through 3 by choosing the best answer.

Most clear, dark nights you can see a shooting star, as we call it, if you keep looking. Those shooting stars are meteors. They are points of light that suddenly appear in the sky, like distant stars, race across the darkness, usually toward the horizon, and disappear.

For a long time nobody knew what a meteor was. But finally those who study stars and the sky decided that a meteor is a piece of a comet that exploded long ago. Those pieces are still wandering about the universe in huge, looping paths that follow the original comet's orbit. There are uncounted pieces of such comets out there in the depths of space. Periodically clusters of them come close to the earth's orbit, or path around the sun. Most meteors are small, probably only a few inches in diameter, but when they enter the earth's atmosphere the friction makes them white hot. Then they look big as stars streaking across the darkness.

There are half a dozen meteor showers each year. Each is named after the constellation from which it appears to come. The biggest of all, the Perseids, named for the constellation of Perseus, occurs on the 10th, 11th, and 12th of August. The next largest, the Leonids, named for the constellation of Leo, comes on the nights of November 14, 15, and 16. . . .

1 Which of the following is the best description of a shooting star?

A an aging star that explodes in the night sky

B a distant comet that shoots across the sky

C the sun's rays when seen in the night sky

D a white-hot meteor that streaks across the sky

2 If scientists observe a new meteor shower, it will most likely be named after

F a comet

G an astronomer

H an orbit

J a constellation

3 Why did the author write this passage?

A to contrast shooting stars with meteors

B to give readers basic information about meteors

C to entertain readers with a story about comets

D to make predictions of future meteor showers

© Pearson Education, Inc., publishing as Pearson Prentice Hall. All rights reserved.

Name ______________________________ Date ______________

Reading Comprehension

from "Up the Slide" by Jack London

Directions:

Read this excerpt from "Up the Slide" by Jack London. Then complete numbers 4 through 7 by choosing the best answer.

When Clay Dilham left the tent to get a sled-load of firewood, he expected to be back in half an hour. So he told Swanson, who was cooking the dinner. Swanson and he belonged to different outfits, located about twenty miles apart on the Stewart River, but they had become traveling partners on a trip down the Yukon to Dawson to get the mail.

Swanson had laughed when Clay said he would be back in half an hour. It stood to reason, Swanson said, that good, dry firewood could not be found so close to Dawson; that whatever firewood there was originally had long since been gathered in; that firewood would not be selling at forty dollars a cord if any man could go out and get a sled-load and be back in the time Clay expected to make it.

Then it was Clay's turn to laugh, as he sprang on the sled and *mushed* the dogs on the river-trail. For, coming up from the Siwash village the previous day, he had noticed a small dead pine in an out-of-the-way place, which had defied discovery by eyes less sharp than his. And his eyes were both young and sharp, for his seventeenth birthday was just cleared.

4 Why does Swanson laugh at Clay?

F Swanson thinks that Clay is trying to trick him.

G Swanson believes that firewood should be cheaper.

H Swanson thinks Clay's trip will be much longer.

J Swanson thinks that Clay is being lazy.

5 Why does Clay laugh at Swanson?

A Clay is nervous about traveling on the ice alone.

B Clay knows where to find a dead tree for firewood.

C Clay thinks Swanson is too old to be camping.

D Clay thinks Swanson is too easily worried.

6 From what literary point of view is this passage told?

F first-person limited

G first-person omniscient

H third-person limited

J third-person omniscient

7 Which of the following is the best evidence that this passage is a work of fiction?

A The places described exist in the real world.

B It describes events that took place in the past.

C It does not contain extensive dialogue.

D The thoughts of a main character are revealed.

© Pearson Education, Inc., publishing as Pearson Prentice Hall. All rights reserved.

Name ______________________ Date ______________

Reading Comprehension

from *Travels with Charley* by John Steinbeck

Directions:

In this excerpt from *Travels with Charley,* John Steinbeck discusses his need to get back in touch with something that means a great deal to him. Read the excerpt. Then complete numbers 8 and 9 by choosing the best answer.

My plan was clear, concise, and reasonable, I think. For many years I have traveled in many parts of the world. In America I live in New York, or dip into Chicago or San Francisco. But New York is no more America than Paris is France or London is England. Thus I discovered that I did not know my own country. I, an American writer, writing about America, was working from memory, and the memory is at best a faulty, warpy reservoir. I had not heard the speech of America, smelled the grass and trees and sewage, seen its hills and water, its color and quality of light. I knew the changes only from books and newspapers. But more than this, I had not felt the country for twenty-five years. In short, I was writing of something I did not know about, and it seems to me that in a so-called writer this is criminal. My memories were distorted by twenty-five intervening years.

8 Which of the following statements best summarizes the passage?

F The author does not believe that his memories are accurate.

G The author feels he has been writing about America without knowing it.

H The author wants to be concise in what he writes about America.

J The author feels that New York is to America as Paris is to France.

9 What does the author mean when he says, "New York is no more America than Paris is France"?

A New York does not represent the truth about America.

B New York and Paris are approximately the same size.

C New York is more like France than Paris is like America.

D New York is more French than American.

© Pearson Education, Inc., publishing as Pearson Prentice Hall. All rights reserved.

Name ______________________________ Date ______________

Reading Comprehension

from *The Story-Teller* by Saki

Directions:

Read this excerpt from "The Story-Teller" by Saki. Then complete numbers 10 and 11 by choosing the best answer.

It was a hot afternoon, and the railway carriage was correspondingly sultry, and the next stop was at Templecombe, nearly an hour ahead. The occupants of the carriage were a small girl, and a smaller girl, and a small boy. An aunt belonging to the children occupied one corner seat, and the further corner seat on the opposite side was occupied by a bachelor who was a stranger to their party, but the small girls and the small boy emphatically occupied the compartment. Both the aunt and the children were conversational in a limited, persistent way, reminding one of the attentions of a housefly that refused to be discouraged. Most of the aunt's remarks seemed to begin with "Don't," and nearly all of the children's remarks began with "Why?" The bachelor said nothing out loud.

10 What in this excerpt indicates that the remainder of the story is most likely to be about the bachelor?

F The story is told from his point of view.

G The aunt and the children are soon leaving the carriage.

H He gets the other characters to react to him.

J He is the most mysterious character.

11 Which characteristic is the narrator referring to when he compares the conversation of the aunt and children to a housefly?

A the housefly's buzzing sound

B the housefly's circular flight

C the housefly's persistent nature

D the housefly's small size

© Pearson Education, Inc., publishing as Pearson Prentice Hall. All rights reserved.

Name ______________________________ Date ______________

Reading Comprehension

Directions:

Read this excerpt from a brochure. Then, complete number 12 by choosing the best answer.

> In communities across the nation, people volunteer and improve the lives of others. Some volunteering opportunities can be found through organizations—serving food in a soup kitchen, working with a group to teach adults to read, or joining others to build houses for those who might not otherwise be able to afford them. In contrast, some volunteering opportunities are not organized. People may take groceries to their elderly neighbors, or a few might get together to help a mother of triplets manage her newborns.

12 What is this passage mostly about?

F why people volunteer

G how people can volunteer

H how people benefit from volunteering

J why volunteer programs save money

Directions:

Read the following announcement. Then, complete number 13 by choosing the best answer.

JOIN THE EIGHTH GRADE DRAMA CLUB!

Whatever talent you have, the Drama Club has a part for you in its upcoming production of Mark Twain's *Tom Sawyer and Huckleberry Finn.*

The Drama Club is searching for the following members:

Actors
Cast members must memorize script and attend all rehearsals and performances.

Set Designers, Artists, and Assistants
Design scenery and props. Attend mandatory meetings. Design and produce stage props and scrim layouts. Drawing and painting skills are required.

Backstage Crew
Members set up and change scenes; construct props; and manage the voice system, curtains, and lighting.

Writers, Editors, and Clerical Staff
Members produce the playbill, posters, newspaper stories, and advertising brochures. Research in encyclopedias and other sources is a required activity.

Please attend our meeting in the auditorium on Friday, March 19, at 3:00 P.M.

© Pearson Education, Inc., publishing as Pearson Prentice Hall. All rights reserved.

Name ______________________ Date ______________

Reading Comprehension

13 Why are writers and editors required to research information in encyclopedias and other sources?

A These members help the people who sell advertisements.

B These members have to persuade the audience to see the play.

C These members must report on how the audience liked the play.

D These members need to create factual materials.

Directions:

Read the following passage. Then, complete number 14 by choosing the best answer.

The recently proposed plan to create a curbside recycling program for the community of Summerstown is a bad idea. It will be very expensive to hire a recycling company to pick up and sort the recyclable materials. As a result, citizens of Summerstown will be required to pay more taxes. In addition, the program may be unnecessary. People who want to recycle may already do so by taking recyclable materials to a local recycling center.

14 The main argument of this passage is that—

F the curbside recycling program is too expensive

G the curbside recycling program is necessary

H the curbside recycling program needs to be stopped

J the curbside recycling program is a good idea

© Pearson Education, Inc., publishing as Pearson Prentice Hall. All rights reserved.

Name ______________________ Date ______________

Spelling

Directions:

Read each group of sentences. For each item on the answer sheet, fill in the bubble for the answer that has a mistake in spelling. If there is no mistake, fill in the last answer choice.

1 **A** The magazine had an advertisement for skates.

B Two buses go to the stadium.

C Cut the paper with scissors.

D No mistake

2 **F** Add that colum of numbers.

G Ling tripped over the door's threshold.

H The traffic noise is a nuisance.

J No mistake

3 **A** Nickel is a metallic element.

B I like watermelon for desert.

C You can use the computers in the library.

D No mistake

4 **F** Rehersals for the play start today.

G A holiday is a happy occasion.

H Liars try to deceive people.

J No mistake

5 **A** Things you own are your possessions.

B Murray usualy eats peanut butter and jelly for lunch.

C The race was canceled because of rain.

D No mistake

6 **F** Jack and Jill had a wedding banquet.

G Please answer the phone.

H The month on the calander is June.

J No mistake

7 **A** It is said that "beggars can't be choosers."

B The baby sleeps in her carriage.

C What is the explanation for an eclipse?

D No mistake

8 **F** There are various toppings on the pizza.

G Carla's bycicle has ten speeds.

H That kite is guaranteed to fly.

J No mistake

9 **A** Choose a catagory: fiction or nonfiction.

B Be sure your answer is accurate.

C Tony got a bruise when he fell.

D No mistake

10 **F** The new student is likeable.

G Sunset will occur at 7:30.

H Jerry plays the bass.

J No mistake

11 **A** Acid rain has a bad effect on the environment.

B Mr. Kelly is chief of police.

C I do not beleive in UFOs.

D No mistake

© Pearson Education, Inc., publishing as Pearson Prentice Hall. All rights reserved.

Name ______________________________ Date ______________

Spelling

12 **F** Dental hygiene keeps teeth healthy.

G It is necessary to brush and floss every day

H A dentist is a physician who fixes teeth.

J No mistake

13 **A** The fallen tree was an obstacle to drivers.

B Nucular accidents are very rare.

C She did not recognize the stranger.

D No mistake

14 **F** A cilinder is a solid figure.

G The flood was disastrous.

H Display your graph on the bulletin board.

J No mistake

15 **A** The quarterback has athletic ability.

B The comittee chose the music for the dance.

C A census takes place every ten years.

D No mistake

16 **F** *Pride and Prejudis* is a book by Jane Austen.

G 100¢ is equivalent to $1.00.

H It takes patience to learn to play piano.

J No mistake

17 **A** The project is easier if you cooperate.

B Are the lines parallel or perpendicular?

C Oak Bulevard is two blocks north.

D No mistake

18 **F** Diamonds are valuable stones.

G Betsy moved to a new nieghborhood.

H The previous month was April.

J No mistake

19 **A** Thomas Jefferson wrote the Declaration of Independance.

B You can return the CD if you have the receipt.

C Heat and humidity make me irritable.

D No mistake

20 **F** The muffins have a pleasant aroma.

G The meeting is scheduled for Friday.

H The movie theatre sells popcorn.

J No mistake

21 **A** Bryce's cold turned into pneumonia.

B Practice will improve your pronounciation.

C Is that a genuine moon rock?

D No mistake

22 **F** Carmen was a defendant in court.

G The flashlight needs a new battery.

H I apologize for interrupting you.

J No mistake

© Pearson Education, Inc., publishing as Pearson Prentice Hall. All rights reserved.

Name ______________________ Date ______________

Language

Directions:

Read the passage. Then, choose the word or group of words that belongs in each space. For each item on the answer sheet, fill in the bubble for the answer that you think is correct.

One of the greatest American artists was Charles M. Russell, ___(1)___ was born in St. Louis in 1866. Russell ___(2)___ to Montana at the age of 15 to become a cowboy, and he never left. By the age of 29, Russell ___(3)___ his living as an artist. During the course of ___(4)___ career, Russell created more than 3,000 paintings, drawings, and sculptures that captured the splendor of the American West. Art critics ___(5)___ Frederic Remington and him to be the most authentic of the western painters. Today, his works ___(6)___ in galleries throughout the world, displayed in the same galleries as works by the world's greatest painters. This is quite an achievement for a Montana cowboy!

1 **A** which
B that
C he
D who

2 **F** moved
G will move
H had been moving
J is moving

3 **A** was making
B will make
C makes
D can make

4 **F** its
G their
H his
J your

5 **A** considering
B considers
C consider
D will be considering

6 **F** hangs
G hang
H were hanging
J will hang

© Pearson Education, Inc., publishing as Pearson Prentice Hall. All rights reserved.

Name ______________________ Date ______________

Language

Directions:

Read the passage. Then, decide which type of error, if any, appears in each underlined section. For each item on the answer sheet, fill in the bubble for the answer that you think is correct. If there is no error, fill in the last answer choice.

> Dear Aunt Jen (7)
>
> I am really looking forward to your visit this summer. We always have so much fun when you are here. Are you ready to go on another picnic down by the creek. I found (8) a great spot!
>
> I have a question to ask you. When I was looking at a box of your childhood toys in the attic, (9) I found an antique skeleton key. It looks so mysterious; I'm dying to know what it's for. My Mother said she (10) had never seen it before. When you visit, will you tell me the storey of the key? (11)
>
> I guess I had better go now, since I have so much homework to do. I just wanted to let you know that I'm looking foreword to your visit. (12)
>
> Love,
>
> Patricia

7 **A** Spelling error
B Capitalization error
C Punctuation error
D No error

8 **F** Spelling error
G Capitalization error
H Punctuation error
J No error

9 **A** Spelling error
B Capitalization error
C Punctuation error
D No error

10 **F** Spelling error
G Capitalization error
H Punctuation error
J No error

11 **A** Spelling error
B Capitalization error
C Punctuation error
D No error

12 **F** Spelling error
G Capitalization error
H Punctuation error
J No error

© Pearson Education, Inc., publishing as Pearson Prentice Hall. All rights reserved.

Name ______________________________ Date ______________

Language

Many people have fond memories of childhood games. What some people may not realize, however, is how old these games actually are. Follow-the-leader dates back to the twelfth century. Others, especially those involveing rhyme, have long histories as well. The rhyme chanted for ring-around-the-rosey, for example, dates back to at least the sixteenth century. Not only do games remain popular over the centuries, passed down from generation to generation, but they also cross National and cultural boundaries. Marbles, hide-and-seek, and spinning tops are only a few of the games, that are played around the world.

(13: childhood games. What some people may not realize, however, is)
(14: especially those involveing rhyme,)
(15: generation, but they also cross National and cultural)
(16: only a few of the games, that are played around the world.)

Although some games go out of fashion and new ones are constantly emerging, there appeal is timeless. It seems likely that the games that will still be played four centuries from now are the ones that have entertained kids' for the past four centuries.

(17: emerging, there appeal is timeless.)
(18: centuries from now are the ones that have entertained kids')

13 **A** Spelling error
B Capitalization error
C Punctuation error
D No error

14 **F** Spelling error
G Capitalization error
H Punctuation error
J No error

15 **A** Spelling error
B Capitalization error
C Punctuation error
D No error

16 **F** Spelling error
G Capitalization error
H Punctuation error
J No error

17 **A** Spelling error
B Capitalization error
C Punctuation error
D No error

18 **F** Spelling error
G Capitalization error
H Punctuation error
J No error

© Pearson Education, Inc., publishing as Pearson Prentice Hall. All rights reserved.

Name ______________________ Date ______________

Language

Directions:

Read each passage. Some sections are underlined. The underlined sections may be one of the following:

- **Incomplete sentences**
- **Run-on sentences**
- **Correctly written sentences that should be combined**
- **Correctly written sentences that do not need to be rewritten**

Choose the best way to write each underlined section and mark the letter for your answer. If the underlined section needs no change, mark the choice "Correct as is."

If you are afraid of spiders, it may comfort you to learn that only two spiders in the United States can be truly dangerous to humans. <u>One is the brown recluse spider. Also called the violin spider.</u> (19) <u>It is a shy creature. Often found among rocks or in unused corners of houses.</u> (20) <u>If you want to avoid this unfriendly little creature, you should know that it is easily identified by a distinct violin-shaped patch on its head and body.</u> (21)

19 **A** One is the brown recluse spider, also called the violin spider.

B One is the brown recluse spider: also called the violin spider.

C One is the brown recluse spider; also called the violin spider.

D Correct as is

20 **F** It is a shy creature, often found among rocks or in unused corners of houses.

G It is a shy creature, often found. Among rocks or in unused corners of houses.

H It is a shy creature. This creature is often found among rocks or in unused corners of houses.

J Correct as is

21 **A** If you want to avoid this unfriendly little creature. You should know that it is easily identified by a distinct violin-shaped patch on its head and body.

B If you want to avoid this unfriendly little creature you should know that it is easily identified. By a distinct violin-shaped patch on its head and body.

C You should know, if you want to avoid this unfriendly little creature. That it is easily identified by a distinct violin-shaped patch on its head and body.

D Correct as is

© Pearson Education, Inc., publishing as Pearson Prentice Hall. All rights reserved.

Name ______________________________ Date ______________

Language

Almost everyone has heard of the unlucky dodo bird. Which has been extinct for a long time. [22] It was first reported in 1598 by Dutch colonizers on the island of Mauritius. The dodo received its name from the Portuguese word *duodo*, meaning "silly" or "stupid." [23] There are drawings and even engravings of the dodo, so we have a pretty good idea of what it looked like. It was quite large. It had short legs. It also had a large, curved beak. [24] However, not much is known of its habits, except that it was flightless. Apparently a dodo would make a nest on the ground, out in the open. In the nest, it laid a single large egg, the egg was at the mercy of whatever might walk by. [25] The last dodo was observed in 1681. They were the victims of careless hunters. They were also the victims of imported domestic animals that destroyed their unprotected eggs. [26]

22 **F** Almost everyone has heard of the unlucky dodo bird. The dodo bird has been extinct for a long time.

G Almost everyone has heard of the unlucky dodo bird, of which it has been extinct for a long time.

H Almost everyone has heard of the unlucky dodo bird, which has been extinct for a long time.

J Correct as is

23 **A** The dodo received its name. From the Portuguese word *duodo*, meaning "silly" or "stupid."

B Meaning "silly or stupid." The dodo received its name from the Portuguese word *duodo*.

C The dodo received its name from the Portuguese word. *Duodo* means "silly" or "stupid."

D Correct as is

© Pearson Education, Inc., publishing as Pearson Prentice Hall. All rights reserved.

Name ______________________ Date ______________

Language

24 **F** It was quite large, it had short legs, it also had a large, curved beak.

G It was quite large, with short legs and a large, curved beak.

H It was quite large and it had short legs and had a large, curved beak.

J Correct as is

25 **A** In the nest, it laid a single large egg and it was at the mercy of whatever might walk by.

B In the nest, it laid a single large egg that was at the mercy of whatever might walk by.

C At the mercy of whatever might walk by, the dodo laid a single large egg. The egg was in the nest.

D Correct as is

26 **F** They were the victims of careless hunters and imported domestic animals that destroyed their unprotected eggs.

G They were the victims of careless hunters and they were also the victims of imported domestic animals that destroyed their unprotected eggs.

H They were the victims of careless hunters, and victims of imported domestic animals that destroyed their unprotected eggs.

J Correct as is

© Pearson Education, Inc., publishing as Pearson Prentice Hall. All rights reserved.

Name ________________________ Date ____________

Language

Directions:

Complete number 27 by choosing the best answer.

27 Which of the following would be the most appropriate tool to help you plan an essay?

A a graphic organizer

B a sentence diagram

C a scoring rubric

D a bibliography

Directions:

The following report contains several mistakes. Read the following passage. Then, complete numbers 28 through 30 by choosing the best answer.

[1]Poets use language imaginatively to create images, tell stories, explore feelings, and suggest meanings. [2]The greatest poets have never made much money from their work. [3]They choose and combine words carefully to enable you to see your world in a fresh, new way. [4]To appreciate and enjoy poetry fully, use the following reading strategies.

[5]Read the lines according to punctuation. [6]Punctuation marks are like traffic signals to a reader of poetry. [7]Then, identify the speaker in the poem. [8]The speaker was the voice that the poet creates to communicate his or her message. [9]Finally, you should try to use your senses as fully as possible when you read a poem. [10]Identify the images that appeal to your senses; and pause to experience and appreciate them.

28 Which sentence does not support the main idea of the passage?

F Sentence 2

G Sentence 3

H Sentence 4

J Sentence 6

29 What is the best way to write Sentence 8?

A The speaker had been the voice that the poet creates to communicate his or her message.

B The speaker had the voice that the poet creates to communicate his or her message.

C The speaker is the voice that the poet creates to communicate his or her message.

D best as it is

30 Which transition best fits at the beginning of Sentence 5?

F However,

G Next,

H Then,

J First,

© Pearson Education, Inc., publishing as Pearson Prentice Hall. All rights reserved.

Name ______________________________ Date ______________

Listening

Directions:

Suppose that the following poem is being read aloud. Read the poem. Then, complete numbers 1 through 3 by choosing the best answer.

Dark hills at evening in the west,
Where sunset <u>hovers</u> like a sound
Of golden horns that sang to rest
Old bones of warriors under ground,
Far now from all the bannered ways
Where flash the legions of the sun,
You fade—as if the last of days
Were fading, and all wars were done.

—"The Dark Hills" by Edwin Arlington Robinson

1 You can tell from the poem that the word <u>hovers</u> means—

A glows

B sinks

C hangs

D flashes

2 What do the "golden horns" sing "to rest"?

F the bannered ways

G the old bones of warriors

H the dark hills

J the legions of the sun

3 What is the mood of this poem?

A joyful

B humorous

C anxious

D serious

© Pearson Education, Inc., publishing as Pearson Prentice Hall. All rights reserved.

Name ______________________ Date ______________

Listening

Directions:

Read the following passage from an oral report. Then, complete number 4 by choosing the best answer.

Wetlands are areas of land on which the water level remains near or above the surface of the ground for most of the year. Types of wetlands include bogs, fens, marshes, and swamps. Wetlands are home to many types of plants and animals, including several endangered species. They also help control flooding by retaining large amounts of water. Although wetlands in the United States are protected by the Federal Clean Water Act and by various state and local laws, many environmentalists are asking for stronger laws to preserve these important water features.

4 This passage is mostly about—

F the Federal Clean Water Act

G the importance of wetlands

H endangered plants and animals

J the importance of controlling flooding

Directions:

Read the following message left on Mr. Jackson's answering machine. Then, complete number 5 by choosing the best answer.

Hello, Mr. Jackson, this is Carla calling from Dr. Avery's office. I just wanted to confirm your appointment with Dr. Avery on September 9 at 8:00 A.M. You should not eat or drink anything for eight hours before your exam. When you arrive at the office, you'll need to give your insurance card to the receptionist. Please call me at 555-1926 if you have any questions. Thank you.

5 In order to dictate this message for Mr. Jackson, you would—

A wait for Carla to call back

B listen only for names you know

C ignore the information that you think is unimportant

D listen carefully to the entire message

© Pearson Education, Inc., publishing as Pearson Prentice Hall. All rights reserved.

Name ______________________________ Date ______________

Answer Sheet for ITBS

Vocabulary

1. A B C D	5. A B C D	9. A B C D	13. A B C D
2. J K L M	6. J K L M	10. J K L M	14. J K L M
3. A B C D	7. A B C D	11. A B C D	
4. J K L M	8. J K L M	12. J K L M	

Reading Comprehension

1. A B C D	7. A B C D	13. A B C D	19. A B C D	25. A B C D
2. F G H J	8. F G H J	14. F G H J	20. F G H J	26. F G H J
3. A B C D	9. A B C D	15. A B C D	21. A B C D	27. A B C D
4. F G H J	10. F G H J	16. F G H J	22. F G H J	28. F G H J
5. A B C D	11. A B C D	17. A B C D	23. A B C D	29. A B C D
6. F G H J	12. F G H J	18. F G H J	24. F G H J	30. F G H J

Spelling

1. A B C D E	4. J K L M N	7. A B C D E	10. J K L M N	13. A B C D E
2. J K L M N	5. A B C D E	8. J K L M N	11. A B C D E	14. J K L M N
3. A B C D E	6. J K L M N	9. A B C D E	12. J K L M N	

Capitalization

1. A B C D	4. J K L M	7. A B C D	10. J K L M
2. J K L M	5. A B C D	8. J K L M	11. A B C D
3. A B C D	6. J K L M	9. A B C D	12. J K L M

Punctuation

1. A B C D	4. J K L M	7. A B C D	10. J K L M
2. J K L M	5. A B C D	8. J K L M	11. A B C D
3. A B C D	6. J K L M	9. A B C D	12. J K L M

Usage and Expression

1. A B C D	5. A B C D	9. A B C D	13. A B C D	17. A B C D
2. J K L M	6. J K L M	10. J K L M	14. J K L M	18. J K L M
3. A B C D	7. A B C D	11. A B C D	15. A B C D	19. A B C D
4. J K L M	8. J K L M	12. J K L M	16. J K L M	20. J K L M

© Pearson Education, Inc., publishing as Pearson Prentice Hall. All rights reserved.

Name ______________________ Date ______________

Answer Sheet for SAT 10

Vocabulary

1. Ⓐ Ⓑ Ⓒ Ⓓ	4. Ⓕ Ⓖ Ⓗ Ⓙ
2. Ⓕ Ⓖ Ⓗ Ⓙ	5. Ⓐ Ⓑ Ⓒ Ⓓ
3. Ⓐ Ⓑ Ⓒ Ⓓ	6. Ⓕ Ⓖ Ⓗ Ⓙ

Reading Comprehension

1. Ⓐ Ⓑ Ⓒ Ⓓ	6. Ⓕ Ⓖ Ⓗ Ⓙ	11. Ⓐ Ⓑ Ⓒ Ⓓ
2. Ⓕ Ⓖ Ⓗ Ⓙ	7. Ⓐ Ⓑ Ⓒ Ⓓ	12. Ⓕ Ⓖ Ⓗ Ⓙ
3. Ⓐ Ⓑ Ⓒ Ⓓ	8. Ⓕ Ⓖ Ⓗ Ⓙ	13. Ⓐ Ⓑ Ⓒ Ⓓ
4. Ⓕ Ⓖ Ⓗ Ⓙ	9. Ⓐ Ⓑ Ⓒ Ⓓ	14. Ⓕ Ⓖ Ⓗ Ⓙ
5. Ⓐ Ⓑ Ⓒ Ⓓ	10. Ⓕ Ⓖ Ⓗ Ⓙ	

Spelling

1. Ⓐ Ⓑ Ⓒ Ⓓ	6. Ⓕ Ⓖ Ⓗ Ⓙ	11. Ⓐ Ⓑ Ⓒ Ⓓ	16. Ⓕ Ⓖ Ⓗ Ⓙ	21. Ⓐ Ⓑ Ⓒ Ⓓ
2. Ⓕ Ⓖ Ⓗ Ⓙ	7. Ⓐ Ⓑ Ⓒ Ⓓ	12. Ⓕ Ⓖ Ⓗ Ⓙ	17. Ⓐ Ⓑ Ⓒ Ⓓ	22. Ⓕ Ⓖ Ⓗ Ⓙ
3. Ⓐ Ⓑ Ⓒ Ⓓ	8. Ⓕ Ⓖ Ⓗ Ⓙ	13. Ⓐ Ⓑ Ⓒ Ⓓ	18. Ⓕ Ⓖ Ⓗ Ⓙ	
4. Ⓕ Ⓖ Ⓗ Ⓙ	9. Ⓐ Ⓑ Ⓒ Ⓓ	14. Ⓕ Ⓖ Ⓗ Ⓙ	19. Ⓐ Ⓑ Ⓒ Ⓓ	
5. Ⓐ Ⓑ Ⓒ Ⓓ	10. Ⓕ Ⓖ Ⓗ Ⓙ	15. Ⓐ Ⓑ Ⓒ Ⓓ	20. Ⓕ Ⓖ Ⓗ Ⓙ	

Language

1. Ⓐ Ⓑ Ⓒ Ⓓ	7. Ⓐ Ⓑ Ⓒ Ⓓ	13. Ⓐ Ⓑ Ⓒ Ⓓ	19. Ⓐ Ⓑ Ⓒ Ⓓ	25. Ⓐ Ⓑ Ⓒ Ⓓ
2. Ⓕ Ⓖ Ⓗ Ⓙ	8. Ⓕ Ⓖ Ⓗ Ⓙ	14. Ⓕ Ⓖ Ⓗ Ⓙ	20. Ⓕ Ⓖ Ⓗ Ⓙ	26. Ⓕ Ⓖ Ⓗ Ⓙ
3. Ⓐ Ⓑ Ⓒ Ⓓ	9. Ⓐ Ⓑ Ⓒ Ⓓ	15. Ⓐ Ⓑ Ⓒ Ⓓ	21. Ⓐ Ⓑ Ⓒ Ⓓ	27. Ⓐ Ⓑ Ⓒ Ⓓ
4. Ⓕ Ⓖ Ⓗ Ⓙ	10. Ⓕ Ⓖ Ⓗ Ⓙ	16. Ⓕ Ⓖ Ⓗ Ⓙ	22. Ⓕ Ⓖ Ⓗ Ⓙ	28. Ⓕ Ⓖ Ⓗ Ⓙ
5. Ⓐ Ⓑ Ⓒ Ⓓ	11. Ⓐ Ⓑ Ⓒ Ⓓ	17. Ⓐ Ⓑ Ⓒ Ⓓ	23. Ⓐ Ⓑ Ⓒ Ⓓ	29. Ⓐ Ⓑ Ⓒ Ⓓ
6. Ⓕ Ⓖ Ⓗ Ⓙ	12. Ⓕ Ⓖ Ⓗ Ⓙ	18. Ⓕ Ⓖ Ⓗ Ⓙ	24. Ⓕ Ⓖ Ⓗ Ⓙ	30. Ⓕ Ⓖ Ⓗ Ⓙ

Listening

1. Ⓐ Ⓑ Ⓒ Ⓓ	4. Ⓕ Ⓖ Ⓗ Ⓙ
2. Ⓕ Ⓖ Ⓗ Ⓙ	5. Ⓐ Ⓑ Ⓒ Ⓓ
3. Ⓐ Ⓑ Ⓒ Ⓓ	

© Pearson Education, Inc., publishing as Pearson Prentice Hall. All rights reserved.

Name ______________________ Date ______________

Answer Sheet

1.	Ⓐ	Ⓑ	Ⓒ	Ⓓ	**31.**	Ⓐ	Ⓑ	Ⓒ	Ⓓ
2.	Ⓕ	Ⓖ	Ⓗ	Ⓙ	**32.**	Ⓕ	Ⓖ	Ⓗ	Ⓙ
3.	Ⓐ	Ⓑ	Ⓒ	Ⓓ	**33.**	Ⓐ	Ⓑ	Ⓒ	Ⓓ
4.	Ⓕ	Ⓖ	Ⓗ	Ⓙ	**34.**	Ⓕ	Ⓖ	Ⓗ	Ⓙ
5.	Ⓐ	Ⓑ	Ⓒ	Ⓓ	**35.**	Ⓐ	Ⓑ	Ⓒ	Ⓓ
6.	Ⓕ	Ⓖ	Ⓗ	Ⓙ	**36.**	Ⓕ	Ⓖ	Ⓗ	Ⓙ
7.	Ⓐ	Ⓑ	Ⓒ	Ⓓ	**37.**	Ⓐ	Ⓑ	Ⓒ	Ⓓ
8.	Ⓕ	Ⓖ	Ⓗ	Ⓙ	**38.**	Ⓕ	Ⓖ	Ⓗ	Ⓙ
9.	Ⓐ	Ⓑ	Ⓒ	Ⓓ	**39.**	Ⓐ	Ⓑ	Ⓒ	Ⓓ
10.	Ⓕ	Ⓖ	Ⓗ	Ⓙ	**40.**	Ⓕ	Ⓖ	Ⓗ	Ⓙ
11.	Ⓐ	Ⓑ	Ⓒ	Ⓓ	**41.**	Ⓐ	Ⓑ	Ⓒ	Ⓓ
12.	Ⓕ	Ⓖ	Ⓗ	Ⓙ	**42.**	Ⓕ	Ⓖ	Ⓗ	Ⓙ
13.	Ⓐ	Ⓑ	Ⓒ	Ⓓ	**43.**	Ⓐ	Ⓑ	Ⓒ	Ⓓ
14.	Ⓕ	Ⓖ	Ⓗ	Ⓙ	**44.**	Ⓕ	Ⓖ	Ⓗ	Ⓙ
15.	Ⓐ	Ⓑ	Ⓒ	Ⓓ	**45.**	Ⓐ	Ⓑ	Ⓒ	Ⓓ
16.	Ⓕ	Ⓖ	Ⓗ	Ⓙ	**46.**	Ⓕ	Ⓖ	Ⓗ	Ⓙ
17.	Ⓐ	Ⓑ	Ⓒ	Ⓓ	**47.**	Ⓐ	Ⓑ	Ⓒ	Ⓓ
18.	Ⓕ	Ⓖ	Ⓗ	Ⓙ	**48.**	Ⓕ	Ⓖ	Ⓗ	Ⓙ
19.	Ⓐ	Ⓑ	Ⓒ	Ⓓ	**49.**	Ⓐ	Ⓑ	Ⓒ	Ⓓ
20.	Ⓕ	Ⓖ	Ⓗ	Ⓙ	**50.**	Ⓕ	Ⓖ	Ⓗ	Ⓙ
21.	Ⓐ	Ⓑ	Ⓒ	Ⓓ	**51.**	Ⓐ	Ⓑ	Ⓒ	Ⓓ
22.	Ⓕ	Ⓖ	Ⓗ	Ⓙ	**52.**	Ⓕ	Ⓖ	Ⓗ	Ⓙ
23.	Ⓐ	Ⓑ	Ⓒ	Ⓓ	**53.**	Ⓐ	Ⓑ	Ⓒ	Ⓓ
24.	Ⓕ	Ⓖ	Ⓗ	Ⓙ	**54.**	Ⓕ	Ⓖ	Ⓗ	Ⓙ
25.	Ⓐ	Ⓑ	Ⓒ	Ⓓ	**55.**	Ⓐ	Ⓑ	Ⓒ	Ⓓ
26.	Ⓕ	Ⓖ	Ⓗ	Ⓙ	**56.**	Ⓕ	Ⓖ	Ⓗ	Ⓙ
27.	Ⓐ	Ⓑ	Ⓒ	Ⓓ	**57.**	Ⓐ	Ⓑ	Ⓒ	Ⓓ
28.	Ⓕ	Ⓖ	Ⓗ	Ⓙ	**58.**	Ⓕ	Ⓖ	Ⓗ	Ⓙ
29.	Ⓐ	Ⓑ	Ⓒ	Ⓓ	**59.**	Ⓐ	Ⓑ	Ⓒ	Ⓓ
30.	Ⓕ	Ⓖ	Ⓗ	Ⓙ	**60.**	Ⓕ	Ⓖ	Ⓗ	Ⓙ

© Pearson Education, Inc., publishing as Pearson Prentice Hall. All rights reserved.

Name ______________________ Date ______________

Answer Sheet

1. Ⓐ Ⓑ Ⓒ Ⓓ
2. Ⓐ Ⓑ Ⓒ Ⓓ
3. Ⓐ Ⓑ Ⓒ Ⓓ
4. Ⓐ Ⓑ Ⓒ Ⓓ
5. Ⓐ Ⓑ Ⓒ Ⓓ
6. Ⓐ Ⓑ Ⓒ Ⓓ
7. Ⓐ Ⓑ Ⓒ Ⓓ
8. Ⓐ Ⓑ Ⓒ Ⓓ
9. Ⓐ Ⓑ Ⓒ Ⓓ
10. Ⓐ Ⓑ Ⓒ Ⓓ
11. Ⓐ Ⓑ Ⓒ Ⓓ
12. Ⓐ Ⓑ Ⓒ Ⓓ
13. Ⓐ Ⓑ Ⓒ Ⓓ
14. Ⓐ Ⓑ Ⓒ Ⓓ
15. Ⓐ Ⓑ Ⓒ Ⓓ
16. Ⓐ Ⓑ Ⓒ Ⓓ
17. Ⓐ Ⓑ Ⓒ Ⓓ
18. Ⓐ Ⓑ Ⓒ Ⓓ
19. Ⓐ Ⓑ Ⓒ Ⓓ
20. Ⓐ Ⓑ Ⓒ Ⓓ
21. Ⓐ Ⓑ Ⓒ Ⓓ
22. Ⓐ Ⓑ Ⓒ Ⓓ
23. Ⓐ Ⓑ Ⓒ Ⓓ
24. Ⓐ Ⓑ Ⓒ Ⓓ
25. Ⓐ Ⓑ Ⓒ Ⓓ
26. Ⓐ Ⓑ Ⓒ Ⓓ
27. Ⓐ Ⓑ Ⓒ Ⓓ
28. Ⓐ Ⓑ Ⓒ Ⓓ
29. Ⓐ Ⓑ Ⓒ Ⓓ
30. Ⓐ Ⓑ Ⓒ Ⓓ
31. Ⓐ Ⓑ Ⓒ Ⓓ
32. Ⓐ Ⓑ Ⓒ Ⓓ
33. Ⓐ Ⓑ Ⓒ Ⓓ
34. Ⓐ Ⓑ Ⓒ Ⓓ
35. Ⓐ Ⓑ Ⓒ Ⓓ
36. Ⓐ Ⓑ Ⓒ Ⓓ
37. Ⓐ Ⓑ Ⓒ Ⓓ
38. Ⓐ Ⓑ Ⓒ Ⓓ
39. Ⓐ Ⓑ Ⓒ Ⓓ
40. Ⓐ Ⓑ Ⓒ Ⓓ
41. Ⓐ Ⓑ Ⓒ Ⓓ
42. Ⓐ Ⓑ Ⓒ Ⓓ
43. Ⓐ Ⓑ Ⓒ Ⓓ
44. Ⓐ Ⓑ Ⓒ Ⓓ
45. Ⓐ Ⓑ Ⓒ Ⓓ
46. Ⓐ Ⓑ Ⓒ Ⓓ
47. Ⓐ Ⓑ Ⓒ Ⓓ
48. Ⓐ Ⓑ Ⓒ Ⓓ
49. Ⓐ Ⓑ Ⓒ Ⓓ
50. Ⓐ Ⓑ Ⓒ Ⓓ
51. Ⓐ Ⓑ Ⓒ Ⓓ
52. Ⓐ Ⓑ Ⓒ Ⓓ
53. Ⓐ Ⓑ Ⓒ Ⓓ
54. Ⓐ Ⓑ Ⓒ Ⓓ
55. Ⓐ Ⓑ Ⓒ Ⓓ
56. Ⓐ Ⓑ Ⓒ Ⓓ
57. Ⓐ Ⓑ Ⓒ Ⓓ
58. Ⓐ Ⓑ Ⓒ Ⓓ
59. Ⓐ Ⓑ Ⓒ Ⓓ
60. Ⓐ Ⓑ Ⓒ Ⓓ

© Pearson Education, Inc., publishing as Pearson Prentice Hall. All rights reserved.

Answer Sheet

Short Answer/Essay

© Pearson Education, Inc., publishing as Pearson Prentice Hall. All rights reserved.